· 中国圣人文化丛书 ·
CHINESE SAGES SERIES

孟子的故事

The Life And Wisdom Of Mencius

编著　蔡希勤
英译　郁　苓
绘图　李士伋

华语教学出版社
北　京

First Edition   2002
Second Printing   2005

ISBN 7-80052-833-2
Copyright 2002 by Sinolingua
Published by Sinolingua
24 Baiwanzhuang Road, Beijing 100037, China
Tel: (86) 10-68995871
Fax: (86) 10-68326333
http//:www.sinolingua.com.cn
E-mail: hyjx@sinolingua.com.cn
Printed by Beijing Foreign Languages Printing House
Distributed by China International
Book Trading Corporation
35 Chegongzhuang Xilu, P.O. Box 399
Beijing 100044, China

Printed in the People's Republic of China

编者的话

　　孟子是中国战国时期的大儒,孔子后一人,有"亚圣"之称。幼年曾得力于母亲的教诲,后受业于子思之门人。
　　本书记载了孟子的出世、讲学、周游列国、著书立说特别作齐宣王客卿时发展孔子仁政主张的故事。一事一图,生动有趣。是了解传统文化,解读孔孟之道的有益读本。

Compiler's Notes

Mencius was the outstanding Confucian sage of the Warring States Period, with the awarded title "the Lesser Sage".

This book recorded stories about Mencius' birth, teaching, traveling and writing, especially about how he defended and promoted Confucius' political opinion. The stories, each illustrated with a vivid picture, are fun to read. Young people will find the book helpful to better understand Confucianism and Chinese traditional culture.

目　　录

1、孟子出世 …………………………………（1）
2、孟母三迁教子 ……………………………（3）
3、孟母断机 …………………………………（6）
4、赴鲁游学 …………………………………（8）
5、孟子学堂 …………………………………（11）
6、孟子师徒游峄山 …………………………（13）
7、天下国家 …………………………………（15）
8、人本性善 …………………………………（17）
9、"四德"与"四端" ………………………（19）
10、舍生取义 …………………………………（21）
11、告子到邹访孟子 …………………………（24）
12、饮食男女 …………………………………（27）
13、孟子游齐 …………………………………（30）
14、一鸣惊人的齐威王 ………………………（32）
15、稷下学宫 …………………………………（34）
16、孟子向威王进谏 …………………………（36）
17、孟子和匡章 ………………………………（38）
18、孟子举荐匡章为将 ………………………（41）
19、坐而论道 …………………………………（43）
20、五霸者，三王之罪人也 …………………（45）

21、进言于诸侯则藐之 …………………… (47)
22、孟母去世 ………………………………… (49)
23、孟子论葬 ………………………………… (51)
24、天将降大任于是人也 …………………… (54)
25、孟子适宋 ………………………………… (56)
26、滕世子拜访孟子 ………………………… (59)
27、孟子适邹 ………………………………… (61)
28、邹穆公问政于孟子 ……………………… (63)
29、孟子讲礼 ………………………………… (66)
30、人皆可以为尧舜 ………………………… (69)
31、然友问丧礼 ……………………………… (72)
32、好善优于天下 …………………………… (74)
33、孟子在鲁 ………………………………… (77)
34、往者不追，来者不拒 …………………… (79)
35、滕文公问政 ……………………………… (81)
36、孟子适魏 ………………………………… (83)
37、治国之道，仁义而已 …………………… (85)
38、享受快乐 ………………………………… (87)
39、五十步笑百步 …………………………… (89)
40、率兽而食人也 …………………………… (92)
41、仁者无敌 ………………………………… (95)
42、白圭难孟子 ……………………………… (98)
43、孟子说作官之道 ………………………… (101)
44、孟子说大丈夫 …………………………… (104)
45、梁惠王去世 ……………………………… (106)

46、孟子见梁襄王 …………… (108)
47、无盐的故事 ………………… (110)
48、孟子在平陆遇孔距心 …… (113)
49、储子见孟子 ………………… (116)
50、齐宣王封孟子为卿 ……… (118)
51、齐桓、晋文之事 ………… (120)
52、挟泰山以超北海 ………… (122)
53、老吾老，以及人之老 …… (125)
54、缘木求鱼 …………………… (127)
55、无恒产者无恒心 ………… (129)
56、孟子谒见齐宣王 ………… (131)
57、居于仁，行于义 ………… (133)
58、周文王的狩猎场 ………… (135)
59、齐宣王问政 ………………… (138)
60、齐宣王见孟子于雪宫 …… (141)
61、"拆明堂"和"行王政" … (143)
62、治国如琢玉 ………………… (146)
63、传食于诸侯 ………………… (148)
64、孟子访管仲墓 …………… (150)
65、孟子谈浩然之气 ………… (153)
66、孟子谈公卿 ………………… (155)
67、孟子谈"三宝" …………… (157)
68、没有规矩不能成方圆 …… (159)
69、天时不如地利 …………… (162)
70、孟子见夷之 ………………… (165)

71、桃应问执法 …………………… （168）
72、孟子谈孝 ……………………… （170）
73、孟子讲"四心" ………………… （172）
74、杯水车薪 ……………………… （174）
75、孟子反对杨、墨学说 ………… （176）
76、箪食壶浆，以迎王师 ………… （180）
77、齐国灭燕 ……………………… （183）
78、各诸侯国以救燕的名义讨伐齐国 … （185）
79、齐宣王说："我愧对孟子。" ……… （188）
80、夫子之道 ……………………… （192）
81、孟子准备离开齐国 …………… （194）
82、孟子称病不朝 ………………… （196）
83、君子不见诸侯 ………………… （199）
84、志士不忘在沟壑，勇士不忘丧其元 … （201）
85、齐宣王挽留孟子 ……………… （204）
86、淳于髡挽留孟子 ……………… （207）
87、要用"道"去援救天下 ………… （210）
88、孟子离开齐国 ………………… （212）
89、如欲平治天下，当今之世，
    舍我其谁也？ ………………… （214）
90、孟子在昼地 …………………… （216）
91、孟子答尹士 …………………… （218）
92、孟子石丘遇宋牼 ……………… （221）
93、孟子在休地 …………………… （223）
94、孟子回到邹国 ………………… （225）

95、重整子思书院 …………………（227）
96、和弟子们研究学问 ……………（229）
97、著书立说 ………………………（231）
98、子产的故事 ……………………（233）
99、孟子溘然长逝 …………………（235）
100、"亚圣"孟子 …………………（237）

◇◇◇◇◇◇孟子的故事◇◇◇◇◇◇

1、孟子出世

公元前390年（周安王十二年）秋八月的一天，孟子父母朝峄山，在回家的路上孟子出生，

因为他生在马车上,故其父为他起名孟轲,字子舆。

峄山即邹山,位于今山东省邹县东南。

据传孟子系"鲁公族孟孙之后",破落后迁于邹马鞍山西麓之凫村。

In August 390 BC, Mencius' parents made a pilgrimage to Mount Yi (in present-day Zou County, Shandong Province). On their way back home, Mencius was born. Because his mother gave birth to him in the cart they were traveling in, his father named him Meng Ke (the character Ke has a radical indicating a cart).

It is said that Mencius was a descendant of the noble and powerful clan of Mengsun. But after the power of the clan declined, his family moved to Fu Village in the State of Zou.

2、孟母三迁教子

公元前386年（周安王十六年）孟子四岁时父亲孟孙激死于非命，孟母仉氏怀抱披麻带孝的

孟轲为丈夫送灵,她决心把儿子培养成人。

凫村西边是一片荒冢,孟轲和小朋友们每天在这里玩耍,他们模仿着大人送殡的样子哭哭啼啼、吹吹打打。孟母看在眼里,急在心里,她把孟轲领回家,给他讲《诗》、《礼》、《论语》和《春秋》,想不到孟子聪明非常,一学就会,学完就跑出去又和小朋友继续玩送殡的游戏。孟母摇头叹息,她认为这样的环境不适合孩子成长,为了把儿子培养成人,她决定搬家离开这里。

一年后,孟母把家由凫村迁到都城西一个集镇上。孟母很快发现街市上的喧嚣声很不利于儿子学习,而且她很快发现孟轲已学会小商小贩们那油腔滑调的叫卖声。孟母没有责备儿子却责怪自己忘记了孔子说的"择不处仁,焉得知?"的话,她决定再次搬家。

孟轲七岁那一年,孟母带着儿子把家搬到都城南关学宫旁边,听着从学宫里传出的朗朗读书声,孟母欣慰的笑了,她知道这环境才是培养孩子理想的地方。

孟母三迁的故事始见于《烈女传》。

When he was four years old, Mencius' father Mengsun Ji died. In heavy mourning garments, his mother carried Mencius in her arms in the funeral procession. She determined then and there to bring up Mencius to be a fine man.

Near their house was an uncared-for grave where little Mencius and his friends often played at holding funeral ceremonies. His mother was displeased at this, and finally kept him at home to teach him the Confucian classics and poetry. Mencius was an intelligent youngster, and he soon mastered his lessons. But he continued to play at presiding over funerals. Realizing that such an environment was no good for her son, Mencius' mother decided to move house.

They moved to a town. But Mencius learned bad habits and uncouth jargon from the bustling market place, and neglected his studies. So when Mencius was seven years old, his mother moved again, this time to a house next to a school in a city. Hearing the sound of reading aloud from the school, his mother smiled with relief that she had finally found the right place for her son's education.

The Life and Wisdom of Mencius

3、孟母断机

孟轲八岁进学宫,由于他天资聪明,而且又从小受到母亲良好的启蒙教育,所以老师讲授的

知识远远满足不了他的渴求。慢慢地他和几个爱逃学的孩子混在了一起,上学时间经常跑到城外树林里去玩,回到家又不得不说谎话。如此再三,终于被母亲发现了。一天孟轲回到家,见母亲面色阴沉,织机上的经线被割断,母亲低声问:"为什么逃学?"孟轲从不见母亲如此伤心,不敢再撒谎,赶紧给母亲跪下说:"孩儿错了……"

Mencius entered the school at the age of eight. He found that the lessons were not up to the standard he had already reached at home, and so got into the habit of playing truant and playing in the nearby woods.

One day, when he returned home he saw his mother looking very sad, and the thread on her loom was broken. She explained that she had broken the thread on purpose to teach him a lesson: By breaking off his studies he was ruining his chances of a fine career, just as she had ruined a fine piece of work.

4、赴鲁游学

公元前368年(周显王元年),孟轲二十二岁赴鲁游学,受业于子思之门人。他曾说过:"予未

得为孔子徒也,予私淑诸人也。"(《孟子·离娄下》)

孟子在曲阜游览观光,尼山、少昊陵、颜母庄、周公庙、鲁桓公庙、杏坛等名胜。

孟子在鲁遍访孔子之孙子思的门人,孟子在一位老人的指引下走出鲁国都城,在山中一茅舍拜子思门人为师。

三年后,老师送孟子下山,老师问:"不知道你回去后,想干什么?"孟子说:"君子有三乐,而王天下不在其中。父母俱在,兄弟无故,一乐也;仰不愧于天,俯不怍于人,二乐也;得天下英才而教育之,三乐也。弟子回去后,欲效法孔老夫子收弟子办学,以传夫子之道。我终生之愿,就是学习孔子,继承其伟业。"(见《孟子·尽心上》)

老师站在高阜之上,目送孟子下山。这时,东方一轮红日正冉冉升起,朝霞染遍群山。

When Mencius was 22 years old, he went to the State of Lu to study with a disciple of Confucius' grandson Zi Si. He said, "I was born too late to be Confucius' disciple. But I can learn from other virtuous men."

In Lu, Mencius visited many famous places in Confucius' hometown Qufu. An old man led him to a thatched cottage on a mountainside outside the city, where Mencius formally acknowledged a disciple of Zi Si as his master.

Three years later, when he had completed his studies, his master asked him: "What do you want to do now?" Mencius replied, "A gentleman has three delights, but to rule the world is not among them. The first delight is that his parents are hale and hearty and his brothers are safe and sound. The second delight is that he feels no shame as he faces Heaven above and the people below. The third is that he can have around him all the talented people in the world and teach them. When I am back home, I'll follow the example of Confucius, and open a school. My life-long wish is to teach our master's ideas and make them better known throughout the world."

5、孟子学堂

孟子从鲁国学成回到邹国后,在多方资助下,经过一年的努力"子思书院"落成了,因为孟子

在当时已小有名气，所以，人们习惯上称为"孟子学堂"。孟子和孔子所处的时代不同，孔子首倡私人办学以来，到孟子时，私人办学已蔚然成风，致仕的官吏以及不愿出仕的士者，纷纷收徒授课，设坛讲学。孟子受徒的原则是："来者不拒"，不问籍贯和出身。另外，他所收的学生都是已有相当学业基础的青年，而不是需要启蒙教育的孩提。

A year after Mencius returned home, the Zi Si School was established with financial support from many people. As Mencius was already quite well known by that time, people liked to call it the Mencius School. Different from Confucius' time, running a private school was in vogue in Mencius' day. Even learned officials received students in their homes. Mencius welcomed students from all walks of life, and most were mature men of learning.

6、孟子师徒游峄山

孟子继承了孔子讲学的方法,常常把学生带出课堂,到大自然中去,以陶冶弟子们的情操。

在一个风和日丽的春日,孟子师徒一行十数人一路踏青来到峄山,孟子给弟子们讲解峄山的神话传说和借机传授修身养性的学问……峄山又称邹峄山,位于邹东南,方圆十余公里。山上奇峰怪石,陡峭峻拔,且多松柏清泉,自古为游览胜地。峄山东峰世传为孔子"登东山而小鲁"处。

Mencius' way of teaching was as flexible as that of Confucius. He often took his disciples out to view the scenes of nature. One sunny day in spring, Mencius led a dozen of his disciples out to Mount Yi. It was a scenic spot well known for its clear brooks and pines and cypresses caressing picturesque peaks. It is said that Confucius once looked down from the summit of Mount Yi, and exclaimed how small the State of Lu looked from there. Mencius told his disciples the legends of Mount Yi and explained Confucius' ideas of how to cultivate one's mind and character.

◇◆◇◆◇◆◇ 孟子的故事 ◇◆◇◆◇◆◇

7、天下国家

孟子对学生们说:"人们常说'天下国家'这句话,可见天下的基础是国,国的基础是家,家

的基础是人。这就是说,每个人的修养如何,不仅是个人的事,而且是关系到国家以及天下的大事。"(《孟子·离娄上》)孟子所说的天下即指中国,国即指中国境内的各诸侯国。故儒家认为"身修而后家齐,家齐而后国治,国治而后天下平"(《礼记·大学》)。

Mencius once told his disciples, "People often talk about 'the empire, states and families'. States are the basis of the empire, families are the basis of a state and individuals are the basis of a family. This means that the cultivation of an individual concerns not only himself but his state too, and the whole empire of China." So Confucians believe that the education of one's family depends on a person's self-cultivation and the ruling of a state depends on the education of each family. Peace and stability can prevail only after the state is ruled properly.

8、人本性善

孟子对弟子们说:"从天生资质看,可以使人的本性善良,这就是我给你们讲的人性善。至于有的人性

不善良,也不是天生如此。"接着孟子讲"恻隐之心,人皆有之;羞恶之心,人皆有之;恭敬之心,人皆有之;是非之心,人皆有之。恻隐之心,仁也;羞恶之心,义也;恭敬之心,礼也;是非之心,智也。仁、义、礼、智,非由外铄我也,我固有之也"(《孟子·告子上》)。

Mencius always held that man is good by nature. He once said to his disciples: "The inborn quality of human nature is good. If a man's nature is not good, it is not because he was born bad." Mencius explained, "Compassion is common to all; so are the senses of shame, respect, and right and wrong. Compassion can lead to benevolence, a sense of shame to righteousness, respect to propriety, and sense of right and wrong to wisdom. Benevolence, righteousness, propriety and wisdom are not taught by others, but are inborn."

9、"四德"与"四端"

弟子万章问:"四德与四端的关系怎样?"孟子回答说:"四端即四心,亦即人之善性。心之官

职在思考，此乃人之所独具，动物则无能思之心。人之善性，用心思考则得之，不用心思考则失之，丧失善性者，则无异于禽兽也。反之，肯用心思考，能加强自身修养者，便可将四端扩张成四德。求满足大体之需要者为君子，求满足小体之欲者为小人。"孟子所说的大体、小体是指修身养性和口腹之欲。

Wan Zhang once asked Mencius about the relationship between the "four virtues" and the "four senses". Mencius said, "The four senses are the senses of compassion, shame, respect, and right and wrong. They refer to the good nature inherent in all human beings. The function of the mind is to think. Only man can think; animals cannot. If he uses his mind properly, a man can maintain his good nature. If he doesn't, he will lose his good nature and be no different from the animals. In contrast, if he keeps using his mind and cultivating himself, he can expand the 'four senses' into the 'four virtues' (filial piety, fraternity, loyalty and honesty). A gentleman strives for the cultivation of his mind, and the petty man strives for the satisfaction of his body."

10、舍生取义

孟子说："鱼，我所欲也，熊掌亦我所欲也，倘二者不可同时得到，取熊掌而舍鱼者也。生亦

我所欲也，义亦我所欲也，倘二者不能同时得到，舍生而取义者也。生命虽然是我所宝贵的，但对我来说还有比生命更宝贵的，那就是义。所以我不做苟且偷生的事。死亡是我所厌恶的，但还有比死亡更为我所厌恶的，那就是不义。所以我不会对一切祸患都取躲避的态度。如果人们只把自己的生命看作是最宝贵的，那么，凡是可以苟且偷生的手段，都可以使用了。如果人们只把死亡看作是最可怕的，那么，凡是可以避免死亡的手段，都可以使用了。然而，有的人却不做为了保全自己生命而不择手段的事，不做为避免祸患而不择手段的事。由此可知，在这些人看来还有比生命更宝贵的东西，还有比死亡更可怕的东西，这就是舍生取义之心。"（《孟子·告子上》）

"I like fish, and I like bear's paw too. If I cannot have both, I prefer bear's paw to fish," Mencius said. "I treasure life, and I also treasure righteousness. If I cannot have both, I prefer righteousness to life. Though life is what I treasure, there is something more precious to me, and that is righteousness. Death is what I detest, but there is something more detestable than death, and that is unrighteousness. So I will not avoid all disasters simply in order to live an ignoble life. If people treasure their lives most, they will try all means to save their lives. If people detest death most, they will adopt any means to avoid death. But there are people who will not stoop to anything just to save their own lives; neither will they stoop to anything to avoid disaster. There is for them something more precious than life and something more detestable than death——they would give up their lives for righteousness."

11、告子到邹访孟子

告子说:"人性犹如杞柳,义理犹如杯盘;将人性纳于仁义,犹如以杞柳制成杯盘。"孟子反问

道:"你是顺着杞柳之性制成杯盘呢,还是毁伤杞柳之性制成杯盘呢?如果毁伤杞柳之性制成杯盘,则亦毁伤人之本性后纳于仁义吗?"

告子说:"人性好比湍急之流,决诸东方则东流,决诸西方则西流。人性之无所谓善与不善,犹水之无东流与西流之定向。"孟子说:"水诚然没有东流西流之定向,难道亦无上流下流之定向吗?人性之善,犹水之就下。人无有不善,水无有不下。当然,拍水而使之跳起,可高过颡额;戽水使之倒流,可引上高山。这岂是水之本性?形势使其如此。人之为不善,本性之改变亦系如此。"

Gao Zi, a 60-year-old scholar of Confucianism and Mohism, once visited Mencius. He said, "Human nature is like an entire willow tree, and! righteousness is like a cup ane plate. Making human nature benevolent and righteous is like making cups and plates out of an entire willow tree."

Mencius asked him: "Can you make a cup and plate without injury to the nature of the willow or do you have to injure it? If you have to injure its nature to make a cup and plate, don't you likewise have to injure human nature to make it benevolent and righteous?"

Gao Zi said, "Human nature is like running water. It will flow to the east if there's an opening to the east. It will flow to the west if there is an opening to the west. Human nature is indifferent to good or evil, just as water is indifferent to east and west."

Mencius responded, "Although water is indifferent as to whether it flows eastward or westwasd, is it indifferent as to whether it flows upward or downward? Human nature tends toward good, just as water tends to flow downward. There is no one who is naturally bad, and there is no water that does not flow downward. Of course, striking water can make it jump up and splash one's forehead, and bailing water can make it flow backward or even up a hill. But how can such phenomena caused by external force be attributed to the nature of water? Man can do evil because his nature can also be changed by external force."

12、饮食男女

告子说:"饮食男女,乃人之本性。仁系内在之物,非外也;义系外在之物,非内也。"孟子问他:"何谓

仁内义外?"告子解释说:"因其年长,故我敬之,恭敬之心,非我所固有;犹雪是白色,故我称其为白雪,此乃外物之白在我心中的反映。故曰义为外在之物。"孟子问:"白马之白与白雪之白,或许并无不同,但怜悯老马之心与恭敬老人之情,亦无不同吗? 子之所谓义,是在于老者,还是在于恭敬老人本身呢?"告子说:"是吾弟,则爱之,是秦人之弟,则不爱也,此乃因我之关系而这样做,故曰仁为内在之物。恭敬楚人之老者,亦恭敬吾之老者,此乃因外在老者的关系而这样做,故曰义为外在之物。"孟子说:"嗜秦人之烧肉无异于嗜己之烧肉,万物无不如此,那么嗜烧肉亦系外在之物吗? 如此以来,岂不与饮食为人之本性的论点相矛盾吗?"(《孟子·告子上》)

Gao Zi continued to discuss human nature with Mencius: "To enjoy food and sex is in human nature. Benevolence is an internal quality, not external, and righteousness is external, not internal."

Mencius said: "Why do you define benevolence as internal and righteousness as external?"

Gao Zi answered, "If I respect someone simply for his seniority, the respect is not internal, because I do not respect him from my heart. It is just like calling snow white because I've seen that it is white. So I say it is an external quality."

◇ ◇ ◇ ◇ ◇ ◇ ◇ 孟子的故事 ◇ ◇ ◇ ◇ ◇ ◇ ◇

Mencius said, "There is probably no difference between the whiteness of a white horse and that of snow. But is there also no difference between sympathy shown to an old horse and respect shown to an old man? Now do you refer the righteousness to an old man or to the man who gives the respect?"

Gao Zi said, "I love my brother because he is my brother, but I would not love him if he were the brother of a man from Qin. It is up to me to decide, so benevolence is an internal quality. Showing respect to both an elder from Chu and an elder of my country is due to their seniority, so righteousness is an external quality."

Mencius did not agree. "There is no difference between the enjoyment of meat cooked by a man from Qin and that cooked by your countryman," he said. "The same applies to everything. Then would you say enjoyment of meat is also an external quality? If it is so, does this not contradict your belief that it is human nature to enjoy food?"

The Life and Wisdom of Mencius

13、孟子游齐

公元前347年（周显王二十二年）孟子四十三岁。齐威王在都城临淄设立稷下学宫，招揽天下文学游说之士，以图富国强兵，霸诸侯，王天下。孟子认为齐威王是一位有作为的明君，所以

决定游齐一展抱负。

In 347 BC, when Mencius was 43 years old, Duke Wei of the State of Qi set up a public school in the capital city, Linzi. He invited all scholars and people of talent to voice their opinions on how to make Qi a rich and powerful state, so that it could dominate the empire. Mencius thought Duke Wei was a wise and promising duke, so he decided to go to Qi to realize his ambition of advising a ruler on good government.

14、一鸣惊人的齐威王

齐威王原是个酒色之徒,执政之初,不修国政,沉湎于酒色之中。每次战争都是齐国失败,

土地被别国占领，人民大量逃亡。有一次淳于髡以隐语对齐威王说："国中有大鸟，止于王之庭，三年不飞又不鸣，王知此鸟为何名？"威王答道："此鸟不飞则已，一飞冲天；不鸣则已，一鸣惊人。"威王开始振奋精神，励精图治，建筑规模宏大的稷下学宫，为的是招揽和选拔贤才。

For some time after coming to the throne, Duke Wei had abandoned himself to dissipation, neglecting affairs of state. Qi was defeated in war after war, and its people fled in great numbers. One day a minister, Chunyu Kun by name, told the duke a story: "There is a big bird nesting in the palace. For three years it has neither flown nor chirped. Does Your Majesty know this bird?" Knowing what he meant, the duke replied, "When the bird decides to fly, it will go right up to the sky. When it opens its mouth and chirps, it will surprise the world." After that, the duke mended his ways, determined to run the country well. As part of his efforts, he had the Jixia Public School built to attract and train talented people for his state.

The Life and Wisdom of Mencius

15、稷下学宫

孟子师徒在稷下学宫住下来，才知道这里聚集了各国著名的学者。邹衍、淳于髡、慎到、环

◇ ◇ ◇ ◇ ◇ ◇ 孟子的故事 ◇ ◇ ◇ ◇ ◇ ◇

渊、田骈、荀况等都曾先后来到稷下学宫。他们和孟子一样来这里并非为了谋食求生，而是为了行道治世。自然这些学者是属于各家各派的。各为其学，各为其道，这里也就形成了一个百家争鸣的地方。

Mencius and his disciples settled down in the school, where they encountered famous scholars from all over the empire, like Zou Yan, Chunyu Kun, Shen Dao, Huan Yuan, Tian Pian and Xun Kuang. They had come, just as Mencius had, to take the opportunity to spread their own schools of thought and apply their ideas to the making of a model state.

16、孟子向威王进谏

齐威王对孟子的学问和学派都非常了解,所以他每次接见孟子是既热情又恭敬,但对他的仁政主张却表现得很冷漠。孟子几乎是天天向威王

进谏，他能言善辩，把他的仁政思想说得上合天意，下合民情，但却终于没能说服齐威王，因为齐威王很清楚依孟子的主张改变不了当时天下纷争的战国形势。

孟子不断向齐威王进谏，企图改变威王的主张；齐威王也不放弃争取孟子，想让孟子成为自己称霸诸侯的谋臣。

Well aware of Mencius' reputation as a thinker, Duke Wei of Qi received Mencius warmly and with great ceremony. But he turned out to be indifferent to Mencius' political ideas concerning benevolent government. Mencius had an audience with the duke almost every day to offer his advice. He presented his ideas on benevolent government eloquently as a policy that would please both Heaven and people. Nevertheless, the duke was unconvinced that in the harsh world of the Warring States a benevolent ruler would survive long. Besides, what the duke really wanted was for his state to become the most powerful one in the empire, and exert hegemony over the others, and he wanted Mencius to help him dominate the empire.

17、孟子和匡章

孟子在齐国和匡章交往甚厚,弟子公都子说:"匡章,通国皆称不孝,夫子与之交游甚密,情同

手足，不怕其玷污夫子的声誉吗？"孟子问："你知道为什么通国都说匡章不孝吗？"公都子说："匡章言父之过，其父不听，逐之出门，父子遂不得见。所以大家都知道他不孝。"孟子说："世俗之谓不孝者有五：四肢懒惰，不管父母之奉养，一不孝也；赌博嗜酒，不顾父母之奉养，二不孝也；好钱财，偏袒妻室儿女，不顾父母的生活，三不孝也；放纵耳目之欲，父母因此而受辱，四不孝也；逞勇好斗，危及父母，五不孝也。在这五项中，匡章有一项吗？他不过是因为对父亲以善相责把关系搞坏了，他不明白'以善相责'只适用于朋友之间，而他错用在父子之间，结果把关系搞坏了。"孟子的言论实际上为匡章洗刷了"不孝"的不白之冤。(《孟子·离娄下》)

During his sojourn in the State of Qi, Mencius became friendly with an official called Kuang Zhang. One day, one of his disciples Gong Duzi said to Mencius: "Everyone says that Kuang Zhang is an unfilial son. As you are so close with him, aren't you afraid that it will smear you reputation?"

Mencius retorted, "Do you know why people say so?" Gong Duzi said, "Because Kuang Zhang accused his father of being wrong, his father drove him out, and they never met each other again." Mencius said, "Usually five kinds of people are considered to be unfilial: First, those who are too lazy to support their parents; second, those who indulge in gambling and drinking; third, those who are miserly with money and dote only on their wives and children; fourth, those whose addiction to music and women humiliates their parents; and fifth, those whose wild behavior endangers their parents. Has Kuang Zhang ever done any of these things? He has bad relations with his father simply because he quarreled with him over what is good. He did not realize that this can be done only between friends, not between father and son." This explanation dispelled Kuang Zhang's reputation for being unfilial.

18、孟子举荐匡章为将

公元前335年,秦国以甘茂为帅攻打齐国,齐廷发生了遣将之争,孟子不为世俗所限,极力

举荐匡章为将,威王用之,果然匡章大败秦军,孟子也因举荐匡章为将有功被齐威王拜为客卿,孟子这一年已经五十五岁。是他第一次取得从政的机会。

In 335 BC, General Gan Mao led the army of the State of Qin to attack the State of Qi. The ministers of Qi were divided as to who should lead their army in resistance to Qin. Mencius recommended Kuang Zhang, despite the fact that the latter was in disfavor at court. Duke Wei bowed to Mencius' suggestion, and, when Kuang Zhang acquitted himself with distinction, promoted Mencius to the rank of Guest Minister. This was the first time Mencius had had an opportunity for government service. He was already 55 years old

19、坐而论道

齐威王、邹忌和孟子坐而论道。孟子说:"规矩是方圆的准则,圣人是做人的准则。作为君主,

应尽君主之道；作为臣子，应尽臣子之道。二者只要取法尧和舜就行了。不以舜事尧的态度和方法事君主，便是对君主的不敬；君主不以尧治理百姓的态度和方法治理百姓，便是害民。孔子说过'治理国家的方法有两种，行仁政和不行仁政罢了。'害民政治，重则身亡国灭；轻则身危国弱。"（《孟子·离娄上》）

Once Duke Wei, Zou Ji and Mencius were discussing the way of good government. Mencius said, "The compass and the T-square are the criteria of circles and squares. Sages are the criterion of human relationships. Both rulers and subjects should observe their proper ways and take Yao and Shun as their models. To serve one's sovereign other than in the way in which Shun served Yao shows lack of respect. To govern the people other than in the way Yao did is to harm them. Confucius said, 'There are only two ways to run a government: by pursuing or not pursuing a policy of benevolence.' An unbenevolent government will bring ruin on the state and its ruler, or at least endanger the ruler and weaken the state."

20、五霸者，三王之罪人也

公元前333年，孟子这一年五十七岁。赵、燕、齐、楚、魏、韩六国在苏秦的组织与参与下，于洹水（今河南省境内）举行会盟，制定"合纵

抗秦"的政策。齐威王以东方大国的身分坐了第二把交椅。齐威王回国后很是得意,雄心勃勃要恢复齐桓公的霸主地位,在庆功宴会上齐威王让孟子说说五霸的情况,孟子说:"五霸者,三王之罪人也!"大臣们一个个要杀孟子,齐威王却笑孟子不识时务。(《孟子·告子下》)

In 333 BC, when Mencius was 57 years old, the most powerful states——Zhao, Yan, Qi, Chu, Wei and Han——held a conference at Hengshui (in present day Henan Province), with the aim of forming an alliance against the State of Qin. Duke Wei of Qi represented the second-strongest state among the six, and saw this alliance as an opportunity for Qi to achieve hegemony, and for himself to become as great as his celebrated predecessor Duke Huan. Back in Qi, the duke held a celebratory banquet, during which he asked Mencius to recount the deeds of the five hegemons in the past. But Mencius said, "The five hegemons were sinners against the three dukes." * The ministers in attendance were shocked, and muttered that Mencius deserved death for such impertinence. But Duke Wei simply said that Mencius was behind the times.

21、进言于诸侯则藐之

孟子回到稷下学宫,公孙丑问孟子为什么有那么大的胆量敢犯众怒。孟子说:"进言于诸侯则

藐之,莫将其巍巍然置于心目之中。当今天下之诸侯,殿堂高数仞,屋檐宽数尺,菜肴满桌,姬妾成群,饮酒作乐,驰驱田猎,随从千乘。我得志,决不如此!他们之所为,皆我所不为者;我之所为,均合古制,我何以要惧怕他们呢?"

Gongsun Chou asked Mencius how he had dared to offend all the grandees of the court. Mencius replied, "I dared to speak out as I did because I despise those so-called dignitaries. They have all built sumptuous palaces for themselves, and idle away their time in merrymaking. They go hunting with retinues numbering thousands. If I had their official responsibilities I would never do such contemptible things. I constantly act in accordance with the teachings of the ancient sages. Why should I be afraid of such popinjays?"

22、孟母去世

公元前 327 年,孟子六十三岁,孟母去世。孟子侍母至孝,决定倾其所有,厚葬母亲。以弟

子充虞监理，为母亲置办棺椁。以卿大夫之礼归葬母亲于鲁。

孟子本邹人，仕齐后接母同住，母亲去世，依礼归葬于邹，当时邹已成为鲁国的属国。

In 327 BC when Mencius was 63 years old, his mother passed away in the State of Lu. Mencius journeyed to Lu, and entrusted his disciple Chong Yu to supervise the construction of the coffin. His mother was buried with the ritual appropriate for a minister.

23、孟子论葬

孟子将母亲归葬鲁国后守丧三年,于公元前324年又回到齐国嬴县(故城在今山东省莱芜市境

内)。弟子充虞说:"承您看得起,让我监理太夫人棺椁之事,当时很忙,不敢打搅您。今天请教,棺木用料似乎太好了。"孟子说:"上古对于棺椁的尺寸,没有一定规矩。到了中古,才规定棺木厚七寸,椁的厚度也与此相称。从天子到老百姓,都讲究棺椁的好坏,这不仅只是为了好看,而是只有这样,才算尽了孝子之心。为法制所限,不能用上等木料,当然不能称心。能用上等木料的人,因为没有财力用不起,当然也不能称心。凡是依法可以用上等木料,而财力又允许的人,都这样做了,我为什么就不行呢?为了死者能够安寝,对孝子来说,难道这就可以满意了吗?我听说过,在任何情况下,君子都不应在父母丧事上省钱。"(《孟子·公孙丑下》)

Mencius remained in Lu in mourning for three years, returning to Qi in 324 BC. Chong Yu said, "I was honored to take care of your respected mother's funeral. But was not the timber for the coffin too expensive?" Mencius answered, "The ancients didn't set any rule for coffins. Later, the thickness of the inner and outer coffins was set at seven inches. From the emperor to the common people, all want to bury their parents in fine coffins. This is not only for appearance's sake, but also because it is the only way to fully show their filial piety. Their descendants would not be happy if the law forbade them to use good materials; nor would they be happy if they were too poor to afford the good materials when they were authorized to do so. Why shouldn't I do the same when everyone authorized and rich enough has done so? What else can satisfy a filial son than making his deceased parents rest in peace? I have heard that no gentleman should in any case economize on expenses where his parents are concerned."

The Life and Wisdom of Mencius

24、天将降大任于是人也

孟子决定放弃在齐国的优厚待遇去远行,弟子们有些想不通,孟子对弟子们说:"舜由农夫中

兴起，傅说出于苦役之中，膠鬲从鱼盐贱役中被提拔出来，管仲曾为囚徒，孙叔敖出身鄙贱，百里奚曾被买卖。所以，天将降大任于是人也，必先苦其心志，劳其筋骨，饿其体肤，空乏其身，行拂乱其所为，所以动心忍性，曾益其所不能。"（《孟子·告子下》）

Mencius decided to take a long journey, leaving the State of Qi, where he had been treated quite favorably. When his disciples expressed their astonishment, Mencius said to them: "Shun was originally a farmer; Fu Yue was a builder before he was selected for office; Jiao Ge originated in the fish and salt markets; Guan Zhong was once a prisoner; Sunshu Ao came from a poor family; and Baili Xi was once sold as a slave. So, we can see from these examples that when Heaven intends to bestow a great mission on a man, it makes him suffer in mind and body. It makes him endure starvation, and inflicts him with poverty, difficulties and all kinds of tests so as to harden his will power, toughen his nature and increase his capabilities."

25、孟子适宋

孟子和弟子们离开齐国都城临淄,原本打算到大梁去见梁惠王,途中听说宋王偃要实行"仁政",就决定先到宋国看看。万章对老师到宋国去颇不以为然,他对老师说:"宋国是一个小国,要

行仁政，如果齐、楚这样的大国因此而攻打它，怎么办？"孟子认为万章提出的问题在学生中很有代表性，就给他们讲商汤伐葛、周武王伐商纣的故事。最后孟子说："不行仁政则已，倘行仁政，四海之民皆举首而望之，齐、楚虽大，有何畏哉！"（《孟子·滕文公下》）

宋王偃是一小国国君，外有强邻侵扰，内有权臣挟持，但他不甘屈辱，虽不奢望称霸于诸侯，却也想国泰民安，富国强兵。因此，他决定实行儒家的"仁政"，所以他非常欢迎孟子的到来。他安排最好的馆舍款待孟子一行，和孟子倾谈三天。但是，孟子到宋国不久就看出宋国大权却被大夫戴盈之操纵，宋王也无能为力。

Mencius and his disciples were on their way to meet Duke Hui of Liang after they left Qi, when they heard that Duke Yan of Song wished to hear Mencius expound on proper government. Mencius decided to go to the State of Song first. Wan Zhang asked him doubtfully: "Song is a small state. If big states such as Qi and Chu wanted to attack it because of its policy, what could it do?" Seeing that his disciples all shared Wan Zhang's disquiet, Mencius told them the stories of how Duke Tang of Shang waged a righteous war against the Duke of Ge, as did Duke

Wu of Zhou against Duke Zhou of Shang. He said, "If the Duke of Song practices proper government, all the people in the world will welcome his sovereignty. What is there to fear even though Qi and Chu seem stronger?"

However, although Duke Yan of Song welcomed Mencius warmly and showed great interest in his theories, Mencius soon discovered that the real power in Song was in the hands of the minister Dai Ying.

26、滕世子拜访孟子

滕国世子（即后来的滕文公）和他的老师然友出使楚国，路过宋都彭城。因为然友和孟子有

The Life and Wisdom of Mencius

旧，滕世子也非常敬重孟子，听说孟子在宋国，就一起去拜访。等他们出使回来，又去看望孟子。世子向孟子请教：如何为君，如何治国，如何服民，如何和大国交往等问题。(《孟子·滕文公上》) 孟子对他提出的问题一一作了解答。

The crown prince of the State of Teng (later Duke Wen of Teng) and his teacher Ran You happened to pass through the capital of Song on their way to the State of Chu. As Ran You was an old friend of Mencius and the prince held Mencius in great esteem, they went to visit him on their way both to and from Chu. At the crown prince's request, Mencius advised him on how to be a sovereign, how to rule a state, how to win the people's hearts and how to deal with the big powers.

27、孟子适邹

孟子师徒正准备离开宋国到魏国去,恰巧这时邹穆公派人来力请孟子归国。邹国虽然是个小国,却是孟子的父母之邦,当时他决定离开邹国

是因为他看到邹国国家弱小,国君又无意实行仁政。所以今天一听说邹穆公派人来,就立即决定回到自己的祖国去。

Mencius and his disciples were preparing to leave Song for the State of Wei, when Duke Mu of Zou sent someone to invite him to return to Zou. Originally, Mencius had left his home state, despairing of its ruler's never adopting benevolent policies. Now that the duke seemed to have had a change of heart, Mencius decided to return immediately.

28、邹穆公问政于孟子

邹鲁相邻,鲁强邹弱,鲁国屡次向邹寻衅,就在孟子决定回到邹国之前邹鲁间已经发生了战

The Life and Wisdom of Mencius

争，邹为鲁所败。孟子一到邹国，邹穆公就对孟子说："在这次战争中，我有三十三位官员牺牲了，而老百姓却没有死一个。我要杀他们，又杀不了这么多；不杀他们他们眼看着长官被杀却不上前营救，实在可恨。您说该怎么办？"孟子回答说："当荒年饥岁，您的百姓中年老体弱的饿死在荒野，年轻一些的四处逃荒，而您的谷仓里堆满了粮食，府库里堆满了财宝，您的官员从不向您报告真实情况。这就是在上位的人不关心老百姓的疾苦，还要残害他们。曾子说过：'你怎样对待别人，别人就怎样回报你。'现在，您的百姓得到报复的机会了。您不应该责备老百姓，您如果实行仁政，您的百姓自然会爱护他们的上级，甘心情愿为他们的长官卖命了。"（《孟子·梁惠王下》）

At this time, the State of Zou had just been defeated by its neighbor, the much stronger State of Lu. The first thing Duke Zou asked Mencius upon his return was: "In this war, 33 of my officials were killed, but no commoners were. Indeed, the common people just stood by watching, and did nothing to help. I want to kill these hateful people, but they are too many. What can I do?"

Mencius said, "During a famine years ago, many people fled, and the old and weak starved to death by the roadside. Yet your granaries were full and so was your treasury. Your officials never reported the truth to you. The common people received no concern from the government, but on the contrary were treated cruelly. Just as Zeng Zi said, 'People will treat you in the same way you treat them.' No wonder the people took their revenge. They are blameless. If you practice benevolence, your people will naturally respect and cherish their superiors, and sacrifice their lives for them."

The Life and Wisdom of Mencius

29、孟子讲礼

　　孟子和孔子一样,无论走到那里总是带着一些学生,随时随地传授知识。有一天,孟子正在

给弟子们讲礼,屋庐子从任国赶回来问老师:"是吃饭重要还是礼节重要?"孟子说:"礼节重要。""妻子和礼节哪个重要?""礼节重要。""如果按礼节得不到吃的便会饿死;而不按礼节却能得到吃的,那也一定要按礼节行事吗?如果按照礼节就得不到妻子,而不按礼节却能得到妻子,那也一定要按照礼节行事吗?"原来,屋庐子在任国,有人用这样的问题问他,他回答不上来,就跑回来问老师。孟子对他说:"回答这样的问题还不容易吗?如果不看清楚基地高低是否一样,而只比较其顶端谁高谁低,要是把一小块木头放在很高的地方,可以使它比高楼还要高。我们说金子比羽毛重,难道说几钱重的金子比一大车羽毛还要重吗?"孟子又从几方面为弟子讲解,最后说:"你回去可以这样回答他:'打伤兄长,抢夺他的食物,就可得到吃的;不打伤兄长,就得不到吃的,你会去打伤兄长吗?跳墙去抢夺邻家的女子,就能得到妻子,不这样做就得不到妻子,你会去抢夺吗?'"(《孟子·告子下》)

Mencius always took some disciples with him wherever he went and gave them instruction along the way, just as Confucius did. One day, when Mencius was discussing the rites with his disciples, one of them, named Wulu Zi, asked him: "Which is more important——food or the rites?" Mencius said, "The rites." "What about a wife and the rites?" Mencius answered, "The rites." Wulu Zi asked again: "Do we still have to observe the rites if we are about to starve to death or cannot get a wife by doing so, but can have both by not observing the rites?"

Mencius replied, "If we compare the height of something without considering its base, then we can put a small piece of wood on a high place and make it higher than a tall house. A lump of gold is heavier than a feather, but is a lump of gold weighing less than an ounce heavier than a cartload of feathers?" He added, "Look at the problem this way: If you had to break your brother's arms to gain food, and you would starve if you didn't, would you do it? Or if you had to jump over your neighbor's wall to take a girl by force for a wife, would you do it?"

30、人皆可以为尧舜

有一个叫曹交的人问孟子:"老师,你不是说过人人都可以成为尧舜一样的人吗?"孟子说:

"是呀，我是说过这话。"曹交说："我听说周文王身高一丈，汤身高九尺，我现在已经九尺多了，为什么还成不了尧舜那样的人呢？"孟子说："这和身高有什么关系呢？尧舜之道，不过是孝顺父母，敬爱兄长而已，你只要这样去做就能成为尧舜一样的人。"曹交听了孟子的解释觉得很有道理，提出想留在孟子门下为徒，孟子对他说："尧舜之道就像大路一样在你面前，难道很难找吗？你回去自己寻找吧，老师到处都有。"孟子授徒的原则历来是"来者不拒"但他这一次从曹交提出的问题却看出此人不可教，故拒绝了他的要求。（《孟子·告子下》）

A man named Cao Jiao once asked Mencius: "Did you say that anyone can be like the sages Yao and Shun?" Mencius said, "Yes, I did." Cao Jiao said, "I have heard that Duke Wen was 10 feet tall and Duke Tang nine feet tall. I'm over nine feet now; why am I not like Yao or Shun?"

Mencius replied, "What has it to do with the height of a man? The way of Yao and Shun is simply to be filial to parents and respectful to elder brothers. Just act this way, and you'll be like Yao and Shun." Cao Jiao then asked Mencius to accept him as a disciple. Mencius told him: "The way of Yao and Shun is like the road. It's right in front of you. Go back, and find the road yourself. There are many teachers."

Mencius had always welcomed anyone who wanted to be one of his disciples, but he refused Cao Jiao because he considered him incapable of being taught.

31、然友问丧礼

滕定公去世,太子让他的师傅然友到邹国问孟子办理父丧的礼节。孟子对然友说:"诸侯之礼,我虽然没有学过,却听说过,应该实行三年

之丧。夏、商、周三代都是这样规定的。"然友回国复命,太子决定实行三年的丧礼,但是却遭到了滕国宗室和百官的反对。他只好让然友再去问孟子,孟子说:"这不能靠别人,执政者好比风,老百姓好比草,风向那边吹,草向那边倒。这种事完全决定于太子。"结果太子按孟子所讲的丧礼处理了父亲的丧事。(《孟子·滕文公上》)

Duke Ding of Teng passed away. The crown prince sent his tutor Ran You to ask Mencius about the proper rites for the funeral. Mencius said, "I have heard about the rites for dukes. They should observe the mourning rites for their parents for three years, as prescribed in the Xia, Shang and Zhou dynasties." When the crown prince decided to observe the mourning rites for three years, other members of the royal clan and the ministers objected. He had to send Ran You back to Mencius for consultation. Mencius said, "It is not up to others to decide. Rulers are like the wind, and common people are like the grass, which bends with the wind. It is up to the crown prince alone to decide." The crown prince followed Mencius' advice.

32、好善优于天下

公元前322年,鲁平公即位,使乐正子治理国政,孟子说:"我听到这一消息,高兴得一晚上睡不着。"弟子公孙丑说:"乐正子很坚强吗?"孟

子说:"不。""他很聪明吗?""不。""见多识广吗?""不。""那你为什么这样高兴呢?"孟子说:"我知道乐正子好听善言。""只有这一条就够了吗?"孟子说:"有这一条治理天下都用不完,何况仅仅是治理一个鲁国呢?假如好听善言,那四方之人会来把善言告诉他;假如听不进善言,那别人只会跟着他说些无益的话,这就会把进善言的人拒于千里之外。进善言的士人不来,那阿谀奉承之徒就会把他包围起来,整天同阿谀奉承的人在一起,能把国家治理好吗?"(《孟子·告子下》)

In 322 BC when Duke Ping of Lu came to power, he let Lezheng Zi manage state affairs. Mencius was so happy to hear it that he couldn't sleep all night. His disciple Gongsun Chou asked him: "Is Lezheng Zi a man of strong will?" Mencius said, "No."

"Is he clever?"

"No."

"Is he widely-informed?"

"No."

"Then why are you so happy to hear it?"

"Because I know he can take good advice."

"Is that enough?"

Mencius said, "With this strong point he is more than capable of administering an empire, let alone the State of Lu. If one can take good advice, people from all over will come to offer it. If one cannot, others will only echo what he says, and those with good advice will be kept far way. With them kept away, flatterers will flock around him. Can anyone administer the state well with flatterers around him all day long?"

33、孟子在鲁

　　果然，乐正子在鲁国执政不久，便派人来接孟子到鲁国去。孟子带领弟子们来到鲁国，鲁平

The Life and Wisdom of Mencius

公决定亲自去拜见孟子,可是却遭到他所宠幸的小臣臧仓的阻拦,鲁平公听信了谗言,放弃了见孟子的打算。乐正子本来想让鲁平公重用孟子,现在只好把真相告诉孟子。孟子说:"我不能和鲁侯见面,这是天意如此,臧家那小子,算得了什么呢?"(《孟子·梁惠王下》)

Just as Mencius expected, not long after Lezheng Zi was put in charge of state affairs, he invited Mencius to the State of Lu. At first, Duke Ping of Lu wanted to call and pay his respects to Mencius himself, but he was stopped by Zang Cang, a favorite of the duke. Duke Ping believed Zang Cang's slanderous words, and cancelled the visit. After Lezheng Zi told this to Mencius, the latter said, "It is Heaven's will that I should not meet the Duke of Lu. So how could that fellow Zang Cang prevent me from meeting him?"

34、往者不追，来者不拒

由于鲁平公不肯重用孟子，孟子想到滕文公当时曾派然友问礼于他，于是带着弟子们离开鲁国回到邹国然后准备到滕国去。公元前322年，

孟子来到滕国。滕文公对孟子十分敬重,把他们安排在上宫住下。可是馆舍的工作人员却对他们师徒鄙夷不屑,当天下午,放在窗台上的一只草鞋不见了,竟怀疑是孟子的弟子偷去了,而且直接向孟子询问查找,问得孟子很不高兴,反问他们:"你以为他们是为了偷一双草鞋才跟我到这里来的吗?"馆舍工作人员说:"夫子之设教,往者不追,来者不拒,难免会良莠混杂。"孟子分明感到这里亦非久留之地。(《孟子·尽心下》)

Rebuffed by Duke Ping, Mencius went to the State of Teng in 322 BC. Duke Wen of Teng highly respected Mencius and had once sent his tutor Ran You to ask his advice. It was arranged for Mencius and his disciples to stay in the Upper Palace. On their first day there, the superintendent of the palace accused one of the disciples of stealing a shoe. Mencius, pained, asked him: "Do you think they came all the way here with me just to steal a shoe?" The attendant said, "Your students are free to come and free to go, and you accept all who come to learn from you. So it's possible that there are weeds among the seedlings." Mencius realized instantly that he could not stay there long.

35、滕文公问政

滕文公问孟子如何治理国家,孟子说:"关心人民疾苦是最当紧的。"孟子建议滕国实行井田制、改变税收制度、兴办学校,从发展教育着手,

实行仁政。(《孟子·滕文公上》)

滕国是一个夹在几个大国之间的小国,要避免亡国,就得恭恭敬敬服事大国。滕文公问孟子:"小国如何服事大国?"孟子说:"滕国虽小,也有五十里,当初周文王兴王霸之业时周国还没有这么大。所以,国家不论大小,只要实行仁政,就能成就大业,为什么只想着服事大国呢?"

Duke Wen of Teng asked Mencius how to run a state. Mencius said, "The most important thing is to take good care of the people." He suggested that the State of Teng adopt the "well-field system," reform the ancient tax system, set up schools to promote education, and practice benevolent government.

Duke Wen of Teng reminded Mencius that his was a small state, surrounded by big powers. He asked him how he should maneuver diplomatically in order not to be swallowed up by one or other of his neighbors. Mencius said, "Small as Teng is, it covers 50 li, making it even bigger than the State of Zhou when Duke Wen started to build his empire. So, regardless of its size, a state will become prosperous and powerful so long it has a benevolent government. Why should you have regard for the big powers?"

36、孟子适魏

孟子在滕国住了三年,仁政主张再次失败。"后车数十乘,从者数百人",浩浩荡荡,向着魏

国的大梁进发,这一年孟子已经是位七十岁的老人了。

魏国由春秋时和韩、赵三家分晋而立国。公元前370年魏惠王即位,十九年后,即公元前362年将都城从安邑迁到大梁(今河南省开封市),所以又称梁惠王。

Throughout his three-year stay in State of Teng, Mencius failed to have his ideas of benevolent government adopted there. So he left Teng, followed by several hundred disciples in scores of carriages for Liang of the State of Wei. By then, Mencius was already 70 years old.

37、治国之道，仁义而已

孟子一行经过长途跋涉来到魏国的大梁，可是，梁惠王对孟子的态度却很冷淡，既没有郊迎

也没有宴请，更没有主动问政。第二天孟子通过关系朝见梁惠王，梁惠王一上来就不客气地问："老先生！您不远千里而来，莫不是对我的国家带来了什么利益吧？"孟子说："大王，您何必说什么利呢？要知道仁义才是最重要的呢。如果大王只想着怎样对我的国家有利，大夫们只想着怎样对我的封地有利，士民百姓只想着怎样对自己有利。举国上下都去追逐私利，国家可就危险了。安邦治国之道，仁义而已，大王何必张口言利谋霸呢？"（《孟子·梁惠王上》）

Duke Hui of Liang took little notice of Mencius' arrival. But finally Mencius secured an audience with the ruler. The first thing Duke Hui said was, "Since, sir, you have come such a long way to see me, I assume that you have some way to benefit my state." Mencius replied, "Why should Your Majesty mention benefit? It is benevolence and justice that are the most important things. If Your Highness only thinks of benefit for your state, the officials only think of benefit for their fiefs and the squires and commoners, only benefit for their families, the state will be in danger from the general scramble for advantage. The way to run a state is by applying the policies of benevolence and justice."

38、享受快乐

孟子第二次见梁惠王,梁惠王正在林苑里湖边观赏风景,见孟子来就不无得意地说:"有道德的贤人也愿意享受这种快乐吗?"孟子回答说:"只有有道德的贤人才能够享受到这种快乐,没有

道德的人即使有这种快乐也是享受不了的。以前,周文王也动用民力修筑高台池沼,但老百姓却很高兴,因为文王肯和百姓一同享受这种快乐。夏桀却与此正好相反,他自比太阳,老百姓憎恨他,就诅咒太阳早日消亡,宁愿和太阳一同死去。做为一国之君,竟使百姓怨恨到这种地步,他即使有高台深池,珍禽异兽,难道能独享其乐吗?"(《孟子·梁惠王上》)

The second time Mencius went to see Duke Hui of Liang, the duke was standing by a lake in his garden enjoying the scenery. He asked Mencius complacently: "Do virtuous men also enjoy this?" Mencius answered, "Only virtuous men can enjoy such pleasure; a wicked man could not enjoy this even if he had it. When Duke Wen of Zhou mobilized people to build pleasure terraces and ponds, they did it happily because the duke shared his enjoyment with the people. The tyrant Jie of the Xia Dynasty, on the other hand, proclaimed himself the sun, but people hated him and wished the sun would soon perish, even if they had to perish with it. When a ruler is hated by his people to such a degree, how can he enjoy terraces, ponds, rare birds and animals himself?"

39、五十步笑百步

通过二次交谈,梁惠王对孟子的仁政主张有了一些兴趣,所以第三次接见孟子就主动问政说:

The Life and Wisdom of Mencius

"我治理国家，可算是尽心尽力了。我考察过邻国的政治，没有一个国家的国君像我这样替老百姓打算的。可是邻国的百姓也没有来投奔我，这是为什么?"孟子回答说："王喜好战争，我就以战争打个比喻吧。战端一开，两军刚一接战，兵士们就丢盔卸甲往后逃跑，有的一口气跑了一百步，有的跑了五十步。那些跑了五十步的兵士耻笑跑了一百步的兵士胆子小，跑那么远，这对不对呢?"

梁惠王说："不对，只不过他没有跑到一百步罢了，其实都是在逃跑，性质是一样的。"

孟子说："这叫'五十步笑百步'，知道这个道理你就不要指望别国的百姓会来投奔你了。"
(《孟子·梁惠王上》)

The third time he received Mencius, Duke Hui, who was becoming more and more interested in his ideas, asked, "I have done my best to take care of my state and people. No ruler of any other state has done as much as I have in this respect. Yet, why do people not flock here from states?" Mencius replied, "As Your Highness is fond of war, let me cite an example from warfare: Imagine that at the start of a battle, as soon as the two armies clash, some soldiers were to throw away their armor and weapons and run for their lives. Some retreat 100 paces, and some only 50 paces. Would it be right for those retreating only 50 paces to sneer at those retreating 100 paces?"

Duke Liang said, "No. Those who stopped after 50 paces fled the same as the others, though they only ran half as far." Mencius said, "If Your Highness understands this metaphor, you should not expect people of the neighboring countries to flock to you."

40、率兽而食人也

梁惠王治国确实与邻国之政有所不同,但在孟子看来只不过是些头疼医头,脚疼医脚的小修

小补而已。所以当他诚心问政时孟子说："农忙季节不征兵,不抽役,保证农民耕种不违农时,这样农民收获的粮食就吃不完了。然后再办好各种学校,使青少年受到教育,这才是富国强兵的正路。可是现在富贵人家用粮食喂猪狗,路上却有饿死的人。"梁惠王说:"这不能全怪我,这是年景不好。"孟子问:"用木棒和刀子杀死人与政治害死人有什么不同?"梁惠王说:"这没有什么不同。"可是您现在厨房里有吃不完的肉,马厩里有用不完的马,老百姓却面有饥色,路上有饿死的人,这就等于执政者领着野兽来吃人。"(《孟子·梁惠王上》)

Duke Hui of Liang was somewhat more humane than other rulers, yet to Mencius these policies were simply superficial measures. So when the duke sought his advice on administration, Mencius said, "If Your Highness did not conscript soldiers during the farming seasons but made things easier for the farmers, people would have more than enough grain for food. Then you could set up more schools for children's education. In this way, the state would become strong and prosperous. But at this very moment the rich feed their dogs with grain, and there are people starving to death by the roadside." The duke said, "I am not to blame, because we had a bad harvest this year." Mencius asked, "Is there any difference between killing people with knives and murdering them with bad politics?"

"No," replied the duke.

Mencius went on, "Now you have more than enough meat in your kitchen and horses in your stable, but the common people are starving to death in the street. Isn't this tantamount to letting animals devour people?"

41、仁者无敌

梁惠王对孟子说:"当初魏国比任何国家都强大,这你是知道的。但从我执政以来,东边败给

齐国，连太子也战死了；西边又败给秦国，丧失河西之地七百余里；南边又被楚国掠去八座城池。我知道这是奇耻大辱，请您告诉我怎样才能报仇雪恨，恢复强大的魏国？"孟子说："您如果对人民实行仁政，减免刑罚，减轻赋税，让老百姓安居乐业，使年轻人受到良好的教育，使他们懂得孝顺父母、敬爱兄长、对人忠诚守信的道理。这样的话，就是用木棒也能抗击秦、楚两国的坚甲利兵了。所以说：'仁者无敌'的话是对的，请您不要怀疑。"(《孟子·梁惠王上》)

Duke Hui of Liang said to Mencius, "As you know, my state used to be the most powerful of all the states. But ever since I became the duke, we have lost territory on the eastern side to the State of Qi——and at the cost of the crown prince's life! Over 700 li of land on the west has been ceded to the State of Qin and eight cities on the south have been swallowed up by the State of Chu. What a humiliation it is! Please tell me how I can get revenge for all these reverses and regain my state's past glory."

Mencius said, "If Your Highness has a benevolent policy whereby he mitigates punishments, reduces taxation, lets the people live and work in peace, and ensures that young people are well educat ed in the principles of filial piety, fraternal duty, honesty and faithfulness, then you will be able to resist the mighty armies of Qin and Chu with mere clubs. You should not doubt that he who practices benevolence is invincible!"

42、白圭难孟子

魏国人白圭,名丹字圭,曾为魏相,是梁惠王心腹重臣。他嫉妒梁惠王频频接见孟子,听说

孟子主张'十分抽一'的税制就故意说:"我想定'二十抽一'的税率,你看怎么样?"孟子说:"你的政策其实就是貉国的政策。假如在一个万户国家里,只有一个人制作陶器,能满足实际需要吗?"白圭说:"不能,那陶器会不够用的。"孟子说:"貉国五谷不生,只生长糜子;无城郭、宫室、祖庙和祭祀的礼节,也没有各国间的互相来往,致送礼物和各种宴会,也没有各种衙门和官吏,所以'二十抽一'的税收就够了。如今居中原大国,取消君臣祭祀和社会间的交往,不设各级官吏,怎么能行呢?因陶器不够使用且不能使一个国家稳定,何况没有官吏呢?所以,尧舜定'十分抽一'的税率是最合适的,想要比尧舜税率还低的,是大貉小貉;但是要是超过尧舜时税率,便是大桀小桀。"(《孟子·告子下》)

Bai Gui was the prime minister of the State of Liang, a favorite of Duke Hui, the ruler of that state and a cunning man well versed in opportunism. He was jealous of Mencius, fearing that the visiting sage would replace him as the duke's advisor. When Mencius proposed to the duke that he should maintain at the traditional ten percent, Bai Gui countered with a proposal for a lenient five percent. Mencius thereupon said, "That is the policy of the State of

Hao. If there were only one potter in a state of 10,000 households, would that be enough?"

"No, it would not," answered Bai Gui

Mencius continued, "In the State of Hao, no grain grows except millet. There are no city walls, no palace or temples, no sacrificial rites, no diplomatic intercourse, and no offices or officials. So a five percent tax is enough. But how could a major state like Liang remain stable without all the above institutions? The tax rate of ten percent set by the sage kings Yao and Shun is the most appropriate. Anything lower would be appropriate for a backward state like Hao; anything higher would make the ruler of Wei like the tyrant Jie."

孟子的故事

43、孟子说作官之道

孟子在魏国是以宾客身份和梁惠王交往的,有一个叫周霄的魏国人问孟子:"古代的君子主张

作官吗?"孟子说:"主张作官。《传记》上说,'孔子三个月得不到君王的任用,就非常焦急,离开一个国家的时候一定带着礼物准备去见新的君主。'公明仪也说过,'古人三个月没有官做就很悲伤。'"周霄说:"这是不是也太着急了?"孟子说:"士失掉官位,就像诸侯失掉国家一样,能不着急吗?"周霄说:"魏国也是一个有官做的地方,我却没有听说过如此急迫找官做的人。既然您这样,为什么您又说君子不会轻易做官呢?"孟子说:"男孩子一生下来,父母便希望他能找到妻室;女孩子一生下来,父母便希望她能找到丈夫。父母这样的心情,人人都一样。但是,若不待父母之命,媒妁之言,便私自相会就会遭到父母及国人的指责。君子不是不想做官,而是讨厌不经正当途径而获得官位。不经正当途径而做官,就像男女私定终身一样为人看不起。"(《孟子·滕文公下》)

While Mencius was staying in the State of Liang as a guest of the duke, Zhou Xiao asked him: "Did gentlemen in ancient times hanker after officialdom?" Mencius said, "Yes, they did. The *Zuo Zhuan* records that Confucius would be very anxious if he was not employed for three months. He always took some gifts for a new lord when he left a state." Zhou

Xiao asked, "Was that not being a bit too impatient?" Mencius replied, "No, a gentleman without a post is like a ruler who loses his country." Zhou then asked again: "In the State of Wei there are many posts for officials. I have not heard of anyone seeking a post in such haste. Then why do you also say that a gentleman will not be so eager for officialdom that he will take any post offered to him?"

Mencius replied, "When a boy is born, his parents want him to get a wife. When a girl is born, her parents want her to have a husband. This applies to everyone. But if the children make such arrangements by themselves without their parents' consent and without the employment of a matchmaker, they will be despised. Although a gentleman wants to be an official, he will not seek the post by improper means. Otherwise, he would be despised by everyone."

The Life and Wisdom of Mencius

44、孟子说大丈夫

魏国有一个名叫景春的纵横家问孟子:"依你说公孙衍、张仪这样的人还不能算大丈夫吗?"孟

◇ ◇ ◇ ◇ ◇ ◇ 孟子的故事 ◇ ◇ ◇ ◇ ◇ ◇

子说:"这些人怎么能称为大丈夫呢?你没有学过礼吗?男人应该居之以仁,立之以礼,行之以义。得志时,和百姓一起走正道;不得志的时候,也能独自坚持正确的原则。富贵不能淫,贫贱不能移,威武不能屈,这才是大丈夫。"

公孙衍:魏国人,著名说客,曾佩五国相印。**张仪**:魏国人,曾游说六国连横服从秦国。

A political strategist in the State of Wei named Jing Chun once asked Mencius: "Do you think men like Gongsun Yan and Zhang Yi are true gentlemen?"

Mencius said, "How can they be considered true gentlemen? Have you never learned that a gentleman should have a benevolent heart, act according to proper rites, and perform his duties with strict honesty? He should always uphold righteousness among the people. Even in adversity, he will stick to his principles. Only he who will never be corrupted by wealth and power, never lose his integrity despite poverty and never yield to force can be called a true gentleman."

45、梁惠王去世

正当孟子向梁惠王游说施行仁政的时候,梁惠王去世了。梁惠王虽然一心想恢复昔日强大的

魏国,但他是一个比较能听孟子游说的国君,他的去世无疑使孟子从政的希望遭受挫折。

While Mencius was still trying to persuade Duke Hui of Liang to adopt a policy of benevolence, the duke passed away. Ambitious as the duke was, he showed interest to Mencius' advice, and Mencius fared no better under Duke Hui's successor in his quest for a position in the government.

46、孟子见梁襄王

公元前 319 年,梁惠王的儿子即位,即梁襄王。孟子见梁襄王后对人说:"远看不像个国君的

◇ ◇ ◇ ◇ ◇ ◇ 孟子的故事 ◇ ◇ ◇ ◇ ◇ ◇

样子,走近他也感觉不到有什么威严。"就是这样一个梁襄王,却也想着统一天下的事。他问孟子:"怎样才能安定天下?"孟子说:"天下归于一统,就能安定。"他又问:"谁能统一天下呢?"孟子说:"不好杀人的国君能统一天下。"孟子认为当时没有一个不好杀人的国君。(《孟子·梁惠王上》)

In 319 BC, Duke Hui's son, Xiang, succeeded to the throne. After his first audience with Duke Xiang, Mencius felt that he did not look like a sovereign from afar, nor did he have any awe-inspiring dignity when observed closely. Yet Duke Xiang's ambition was to rule the whole world! He asked Mencius: "How can I make the world stable?" Mencius said, "Once it is unified, it will be stable."

"But who can unify the world?" asked the duke.

Mencius replied, "He who will not kill good men can unify the world." At that time there seemed to be no ruler who did not revel in slaughter.

47、无盐的故事

孟子既然认为梁襄王不能实行"仁政",他决计离开魏国。这时孟子听说齐宣王即位以后,颇

想有所作为，因此他即位后第一件事就是振兴稷下学宫，公开礼聘天下学者贤士，一时天下学者贤士不下千人云集临淄。孟子决定再次到齐国去，还因为他听到一个"无盐的故事"，说齐国无盐邑有个出名的丑女，名叫钟离春，四十岁不得出嫁，自谒齐宣王，当面指责其奢淫腐败，并陈述齐国危难四点，齐宣王竟大受感动，不仅全部采纳她的政治主张还把她立为王后。发誓励精图治，振兴齐国。孟子感到齐宣王正是自己要找的"明君"。孟子一行向齐国进发，路上正巧遇到齐国王子狩猎的马队，像山洪爆发一样横冲过来，孟子师徒赶紧把车辆靠路边停下。孟子看着傲慢无礼的王子不禁摇头叹惜说："居移气，养移体，大哉居乎！"（《孟子·尽心上》）

Mencius decided to leave Liang, because he saw that Duke Xiang had no intention of adopting a policy of benevolence. He heard that Duke Xuan of the State of Qi was a wise duke. The first thing Duke Xuan did after taking power was to revitalize the Jixia School and invite scholars and able men from all over the empire to teach there. But what made Mencius finally decide to go to Qi was the story of the girl of Wuyan County:

There was a girl in Wuyan County named Zhong

Lichun. She was so plain-looking that she was not married off although she was 40 years old. She asked for an audience with Duke Xuan, and criticized him to his face for living in extravagance and debauchery, pointing out four dangers that threatened the State of Qi. The duke was so impressed by her insights that he made her his queen and his closest advisor.

48、孟子在平陆遇孔距心

孟子一行来到齐国南疆边城平陆,孟子每到一地有入境问俗,勤于考察,慰民疾苦的习惯。

The Life and Wisdom of Mencius

这次到了平陆,他也四处走走看看,了解到一些实际情况,当晚他和平陆地方长官孔距心作了一次深谈。他问孔距心说:"如果你的士兵一天之中三次失职,你会开除他吗?"孔距心说:"不必等三次,我就开除他了。"孟子说:"那么,你自己失职的地方也很多。灾荒年成,你辖区的百姓,年老体弱者抛尸荒野,年轻体壮的逃亡四方,这样的人快有一千人了吧!"孔距心分辨说:"这是天灾,不是我个人的力量所能抗拒的。"孟子说:"譬如说现在有一个人,替人放牧牛羊,但他却找不到牧场和草料,那他是把牛羊退还给主人呢?还是眼看着牛羊一个个饿死呢?"孔距心说:"你这样比喻就是我的罪过了。"

过了些时,孟子朝见齐王时说:"你的地方长官中我认识五位,能够知道自己罪过的只有孔距心一个。"他把以前和孔距心的谈话又说了一遍。齐王听后说:"这也是我的罪过。"(《孟子·公孙丑下》)

Everywhere Mencius went, he would investigate the local customs, and ask about the people's livelihood. Arriving in Pinglu, a small town in Qi, Mencius had a long talk with the local magistrate, Kong Juxin. Mencius asked him: "Would you dismiss a soldier if he neglected his duty three times in one day?" Kong Juxin said, "I would dismiss him even before he erred three times this way." Mencius then said, "You yourself have failed to do many of your duties. During famines, the corpses of the old and weak can be found scattered in the wilderness, and the young and strong have fled in droves to other areas." Kong Juxin protested, "This was the result of natural disasters; I could do nothing to prevent it." Mencius asked again: "If a man herding cattle or sheep for another fails to find pasture or forage for them, should he return the cattle or sheep to the owner, or should he watch them die one by one from starvation?" Kong Juxin thereupon admitted, "Now I know it was my fault."

Some time later, Mencius had an audience with the Duke Xuan of Qi, and said: "I have made the acquaintance of five of your local officials, and only Kong Juxin could admit his fault." Then he told the duke of his conversation with Kong Juxin. After hearing this, the duke said, "I too was at fault."

49、储子见孟子

孟子告别了孔距心离开平陆向齐国都城临淄进发,远远看见一辆马车飞奔而来,来到跟前才

孟子的故事

知道是齐相储子的家人带着厚礼来迎接孟子。孟子一行跟随来人直接住进稷下学宫,少顷齐相储子来看孟子。储子说:"王曾派人来窥探您,您真有和别人不同的地方吗?"孟子微微一笑说:"你看我有什么和别人不一样的地方吗?其实,就是尧舜也没有什么与人不同的地方。"(《孟子·离娄下》)

Bidding farewell to Kong Juxin, Mencius and his disciples left Pinglu to go to Linzhi, capital of Qi. They saw a carriage approaching at great speed from a distance. When it stopped before them they realized that it belonged to the prime minister of Qi, Chu Zi, who had sent his steward to meet them with expensive gifts. Mencius and his followers were escorted to the Jixia School. Before long, Chu Zi himself called. The prime minister asked, "Do you really have anything different from those of other scholars?" Mencius smiled, and said, "Do you perceive anything peculiar about me? Actually, even Yao and Shun were no different from the common people."

50、齐宣王封孟子为卿

孟子到稷下学宫的第二天,齐宣王率领文武百官在王宫东门外举行隆重的欢迎仪式,旌旗

猎猎,礼炮轰鸣,场面热烈肃穆……齐宣王封孟子为卿,仪式之后齐宣王亲往学宫拜访孟子,孟子受宠若惊,给齐宣王讲"保民而王,莫之能御也"的道理。其实,孟子根本没弄明白齐宣王欢迎他的目的。

The day after Mencius and his disciples settled down in Jixia School, Duke Xuan of Qi held a grand ceremony attended by all his ministers outside his palace's east gate to welcome Mencius. The duke solemnly conferred the title of minister upon Mencius, and called on him at the Jixia School right after the ceremony. Mencius was overwhelmed by these favors, and eagerly explained to him his idea that a ruler would be invincible if he did his best to protect his people. However, Mencius did not know that the ambition of Duke Xuan of Qi was to make himself the most powerful ruler in China by any means, fair or foul.

51、齐桓、晋文之事

孟子这次回到齐国没有想到会受到齐宣王如此隆重的款待,他不禁想到实现自己的政治抱负

的时机终于来到了。其实,就在孟子回到齐国之前,列国间的局势发生了新的变化。韩、赵、魏、燕、楚五国联合抗秦,结果在函谷关战败。这一仗动摇了强秦和东方列国之间的均势局面,也刺激了齐宣王励精图治的决心。这是齐宣王召唤和厚待孟子的主要原因,所以他第一次会见孟子就迫不及待地问孟子:"您可以给我讲讲齐桓公、晋文公称霸诸侯的事吗?"孟子回答说:"孔子的学生们没有谈到过齐桓公、晋文公的事,所以没有传下来,我也不曾听说过。您如果一定让我说,我就说说用道德的力量统一天下的'王道'吧!"

The first thing Duke Xuan asked Mencius was: "Can you tell me how Duke Huan of Qi and Duke Wen of Jin became the hegemons of the states in their time?" Mencius said, "The disciples of Confucius never mentioned anything about them, nor have I ever heard anything about them. If Your Highness really wants me to tell something useful, let me talk about the way of governance that can unify the world with the power of virtue."

The Life and Wisdom of Mencius

52、挟泰山以超北海

齐宣王想知道齐桓公、晋文公称霸诸侯的事，实际上是想让孟子辅助他成就霸业。而孟子却极

力劝他实行王道，齐宣王只好说："要有什么样的道德才能统一天下呢？"孟子说："如果是为着老百姓生活安定去统一天下，是没有人能够阻挡得了的。"齐宣王问："像我这样的人可以吗？""可以。我曾听说你对祭钟杀一头牛都不忍心，要求杀一只羊代替。虽然老百姓说你以羊换牛是吝啬，可我知道您是不忍。一个有不忍之心的国君就能统一天下。"

齐宣王对孟子的仁政主张没有太大的兴趣，但又对孟子抱着太大的希望，就一再强调自己做不到。孟子对齐宣王说："如果你说挟起泰山跨越北海的事做不到，这是真的做不到。但如果说为老人折取树枝的事我做不到，这是不肯去做，而不是做不到。所以，您的不行仁政不是做不到，而是不肯去做。"（《孟子·梁惠王上》）

"What kind of virtue can unify the world?" asked the duke. Mencius replied, "No one can stop Your Highness if you are determined to unify the world to create a prosperous and peaceful life for its people." The duke asked, "Can I do it?" Mencius assured him that he could, explaining, "I have heard that you ordered that a sheep be substituted for a cow at a certain sacrifice. People said that you did so in order to save expense. But I know that you could not bear to hear the cow bellowing in fear as it was being led to the slaughter. A sovereign with a kind heart like yours can surely unify the world."

The Duke did not have much interest in Mencius' idea of virtue, but still needed his help. He protested that following the way of virtue was too difficult, but Mencius said, "If Your Highness said that you could not carry Mount Tai under your arm and carry it across the North Sea, it would be true. But to say that you cannot break a branch to make a stick for an elderly person, it would not be true. So it is not that you are unable to practice the way of virtue, but that you are unwilling to do so."

53、老吾老,以及人之老

孟子对齐宣王说:"老吾老,以及人之老;幼吾幼,以及人之幼。如果治理国家能从这一原则

出发,统一天下则易如反掌。"(《孟子·梁惠王上》)

孟子说:"由尊敬自己的老人,从而推广到尊敬所有的老人;爱护自己的儿女,从而推广到爱护所有人家的儿女。如果治理国家能从这一原则出发,统一天下则易如反掌。"

Mencius said to Duke Xuan of Qi: "Respect your own parents and do the same to others' parents; love your own children and extend your love to all children. If Your Highness can rule the state with this principle, then unifying the world will be as easy as turning your hand over."

54、缘木求鱼

孟子问齐宣王最大的欲望是什么？齐宣王只是笑而不答。孟子想了想说："那我知道您最大的

愿望是什么了。您是想扩张疆土，使秦、楚这样的大国都臣服于您，自己做天下的盟主，同时再收服四周的其他民族。不过，以您现在的作为来实现您的欲望，无疑是缘木求鱼罢了。"孟子又说："缘木求鱼，虽然捉不到鱼，却不至于有什么祸患。以您现在的做法来实现您的愿望，不但达不到目的，而且必然后患无穷。"（《孟子·梁惠王上》）

Mencius asked Duke Xuan of Qi what he wanted most. The duke just smiled. Mencius thought a little, and said, "I know what it is. Your Highness wants to expend your territory, and be the hegemon of all the states, so that the big powers like Qin and Chu will be under your control and all the other people will be your subjects. But that ambition is like trying to catch fish by climbing a tree." Mencius went on, "One doesn't incur disaster if he can't catch fish in a tree. If Your Highness wants to realize his ambition by doing things like this, not only will he not succeed, but he will bring about endless trouble in the future."

55、无恒产者无恒心

孟子对齐宣王说:"无恒产者无恒心,所以贤明的君主要使百姓的产业收入上可以赡养父母,

下足以抚养妻子儿女;好年成可以丰衣足食,坏年成也不至于饿死。然后再教育他们,老百姓自然就容易接受。现在的情况是老百姓的产业收入上不够赡养父母,下不足以抚养妻子儿女,好年成尚且难以温饱,坏年成只有死路一条了。老百姓连生命都保不住,哪里有闲工夫学习礼仪呢?"(《孟子·梁惠王上》)

Mencius told Duke Xuan of Qi: "If people possess no property and have no regular income, they will not have any moral confidence. So a wise ruler will see to it that the common people have enough income from the land to support their parents and family. They will have abundant food and clothing in years of good harvest and will not starve after a bad harvest. Only then will people care for education. But now the people do not have enough income from the land to support their families. They barely have enough to feed and clothe themselves, and perish in years of bad harvests. When people can hardly survive, how can they afford to pay attention to the rites?"

56、孟子谒见齐宣王

孟子谒见齐宣王说:"听说陛下爱好音乐,故今日来请教。"齐宣王不好意思地说:"我不具备

爱好先王古典音乐的条件,只是爱好民间世俗音乐罢了。"孟子说:"其实音乐都是一样的,只要你爱好音乐,那齐国就有大治的希望了。"齐宣王问:"这是为什么?"孟子问:"你是一个人欣赏音乐快乐,还是和大家一起欣赏音乐快乐?"齐宣王不明白孟子的意思,只好说:"当然是和大家一起欣赏音乐快乐。"孟子说:"如果您能和老百姓一同快乐,天下就大治了。"(《孟子·梁惠王下》)

Mencius told Duke Xuan: "I heard that Your Highness likes music, so I came today to ask for advice." The duke demurred. "I am not naturally adept at classical music, as my ancestors were," he said. "I am merely able to appreciate some folk tunes." Mencius said, "Regardless of whether you like classical or popular music, so long as you like music there is hope for the State of Qi." He went on, "Do you prefer to enjoy music by yourself or with other people?" The duke said, "Of course, there is more enjoyment listening to music in the company of others." Mencius said, "In that case, if you can share happiness with the common people, then you can rule the world."

57、居于仁,行于义

齐王子垫是个放荡不羁的花花公子,齐宣王令王子拜孟子为师,请孟子教他成人。王子问:"读书人应

该干什么?"孟子说:"使自己的志行高尚。"王子问:"怎样才能使自己志行高尚?"孟子说:"行仁义而已。杀一无辜者,非仁也;非己所有而取之,非义也。所居何处? 仁也;所行之路在何处? 义也。居于仁,行于义,大人的工作便齐备了。"(《孟子·尽心上》)

Prince Dian was rather dissipated in his conduct, so his father Duke Xuan of Qi made him to take Mencius as his tutor.

Prince Dian asked Mencius, "What should a scholar do?" Mencius said, "He should make himself noble in mind and conduct." The prince asked again: "How can I achieve this?" Mencius explained, "Just be benevolent and righteous in everything you do. It is not benevolent to kill an innocent person, and it is not righteous to take anything that is not yours. Keep to the principle of benevolence, and follow the road of righteousness. Then you can meet the requirements of a noble man."

孟子的故事

58、周文王的狩猎场

齐宣王问孟子:"听说周文王有一处方七十里的狩猎场,有这事吗?"孟子说:"史书上有这样

The Life and Wisdom of Mencius

的记载。"齐宣王问："真有这么大吗?"孟子说："老百姓还嫌太小呢。"齐宣王说："我的狩猎场才不过四十里,老百姓却认为太大了,这是为什么?"孟子说："文王的狩猎场虽然有七十里大,但割草打柴的可以进去,捕鸟捉兽的人也可以进去,文王和老百姓共同使用这个狩猎场,自然就显得小了。可是你的狩猎场虽然只有四十里大,老百姓却不可以进去砍柴和打猎,违禁者处死。这四十里狩猎场对老百姓来说,无疑是一个陷井。他们当然嫌这个狩猎场太大了。"(《孟子·梁惠王下》)

Duke Xuan of Qi said to Mencius: "I have heard that Duke Wen of Zhou had a hunting park of 70 square li. Is it true?" Mencius answered, "Yes, it is so recorded in the history books." The duke asked, "Was it really so big?" Mencius said, "Yes, and people thought it was not big enough." The duke was puzzled, "My hunting park is no more than 40 square li, and yet people say that it is too big. Why?" Mencius replied, "Though Duke Wen's hunting park was 70 square li, woodcutters and hunters could go there freely. All the people could use it, together with the duke. So it was considered not big enough. But your hunting park, though it is only 40 square li, is out of bounds to the common people. For them, it is like a trap because they will be executed if they step into it. So of course they complain that it is too big."

59、齐宣王问政

齐宣王问:"和邻国交往有什么必须遵循的原则吗?"孟子说:"有的。仁德的人可以以大事小,

所以商汤曾服事葛伯，文王曾服事昆夷。聪明的人可以以小事大，所以太王曾服事熏育，勾践曾服事夫差。以大事小的人能够随遇而安；以小事大的人谨小慎微。随遇而安的人可以安定天下；谨小慎微的人可以保全自己的国家。"

齐宣王说："我崇尚勇武，恐怕难以服事别国。"孟子说："勇有大勇和小勇，小勇乃匹夫之勇，不过敌一人而已。大勇就像周文王一样一怒而安天下之民。如果您能有文王之勇，天下百姓都会拥护你的。"（《孟子·梁惠王下》）

Duke Xuan asked Mencius: "Are there any principles for dealing with neighboring dukedoms?" Mencius replied, "Yes. A benevolent man could serve those who are weaker, just like Tang of Shang served Count Ge and Duke Wen served Kun Yi. * A wise man could serve those who are stronger, just like Duke Tai served Xun Yu * * and Gou Jian served Fu Chai. * * * The strong who serve the weak can easily adapt themselves to circumstances, and keep the world at peace. The weak who serve the strong must be very cautious so as to keep their states safe."

Duke Xuan said, "I believe in force and courage. I can hardly serve other states." Mencius said, "There is small courage and great courage.

With small courage, one can defeat only one enemy. Duke Wen of Zhou displayed great courage, and so he was able to bring peace to all the people in the world. Once you have the courage of Duke Wen you will have the support of all the people."

* Ge and Kun Yi were small states later wiped out by the ones which had once served them. Tang established the Shang Dynasty, and Wen established the Zhou Dynasty.

* * Duke Tai was the grandfather of Duke Wen. Xun Yu was a powerful northern tribe.

* * * Gou Jian was once defeated by Fu Chai. He offered to serve Fu Chai, and eventually defeated him.

60、齐宣王见孟子于雪宫

齐宣王在他的"别墅"里会见孟子。齐宣王问:"有才德的人也有这种游乐吗?"孟子说:"有

的。如果他们得不到这种游乐,就会埋怨国君的。因为国君应该和他的百姓同享这种快乐。如果国君以百姓的快乐为自己的快乐,百姓也会以国君的快乐为自己的快乐。如果国君能以百姓的忧愁为自己的忧愁,那百姓就会以国君的忧愁为自己的忧愁。"(《孟子·梁惠王下》)

Duke Xuan received Mencius at his Snow Palace. The duke asked him: "Do virtuous men also enjoy such entertainment?" Mencius replied, "Yes. If they could not get such enjoyment they would blame the duke, because the duke should share his delights with his people. If a sovereign takes the happiness of his people as his own, the people will take his happiness as their own. If he takes their sorrows as his own, the people will likewise take his sorrows as their own."

◇◇◇◇◇◇孟子的故事◇◇◇◇◇◇

61、"拆明堂"和"行王政"

齐宣王问孟子:"别人都劝我拆毁明堂,你说是拆还是不拆?"孟子说:"明堂是有德政而又能

统一天下的君主施王政的地方。您如果想实行王政，就不要拆毁它。"齐宣王问："怎样实行王政?"孟子说："像周文王治理周国那样实行王政。"

齐宣王又问孟子："商汤放桀，武王伐纣，真有其事吗?"孟子说："史书上有这样的记载。"齐宣王说："作臣子的杀掉君主，这应该吗?"孟子说："败坏仁政的人叫'贼'，破坏道义的人叫'残'，残贼之人叫'独夫'。我只听说周武王诛杀独夫商纣，没有听说过他是以臣弑君。"(《孟子·梁惠王下》)

Duke Xuan said to Mencius: "Many people have said that I should pull down the Great Hall. What do you think?" Mencius replied, "The Great Hall is a place where a benevolent duke rules in the way of righteous monarchs to unify the world. If you want to practice the policy of benevolence, do not pull it down." The duke asked, "How can I rule in the way of righteous monarchs?" Mencius said, "Just rule the state as Duke Wen of Zhou did, and practice the policy of benevolence."

Duke Xuan asked again: "Is it true that Tang of Shang exiled Jie and Duke Wu sent an expedition against Zhou?" Mencius replied, "It is so recorded in the history books." The duke said, "Is it right for an official to kill his ruler?" Mencius replied, "I have heard that Duke Wu of Zhou killed an autocrat who was cruel and immoral, but I have never heard that he killed his ruler."

The Life and Wisdom of Mencius

62、治国如琢玉

孟子对齐宣王说:"好比您有一块上好的璞玉,虽然很贵重,但必经玉匠把它雕琢成器皿才

有价值。至于治理国家,你只要求大臣们按你的话去做,这和要玉匠按你的办法去雕琢玉石有什么区别呢?"

孟子得宠于齐宣王,齐国上下无人不知。但孟子心里明白,宣王只是把他作为一件摆设,至于孟子所主张的仁政齐宣王是不会实行的。

Mencius drew an analogy for Duke Xuan, as follows: "Suppose you have a high-quality jade. It is precious, but you have to make craftsmen carve it first. This is no different from ruling a state, when you have to tell your ministers what to do and how to do it."

The people of the State of Qi all thought that Mencius had the favor of Duke Xuan. But Mencius knew clearly that the duke only pretended to listen to his advice, and used him as a mere ornament for his court.

The Life and Wisdom of Mencius

63、传食于诸侯

弟子彭更问老师:"我们师徒长期住在国外,为谋道而到处奔走,夫子后车数十乘,弟子数百

人,传食于诸侯,不是太过分了吗?"孟子说:"各种工匠以自己的产品谋饭吃,君子研究学问,推行王道怎么能说是为了谋饭吃呢?如果不合理,一顿饭也不可以接受。如果合理,舜接受了尧的天下,也不为过分——你以为我们过分了吗?"(《孟子·滕文公下》)

The disciple Peng Geng said to Mencius: "We have been travelling so long around the states to promote the ways of the ancient sage rulers. Is it not extravagant of you to have hundreds of disciples travelling in dozens of carriages, accepting hospitality from one lord after another?" Mencius answered, "Craftsmen work for food only. But how can gentlemen study and promote the way of righteous government for food only? I would not accept even one meal if it did not come the right way. It was not excessive for Shun to accept the whole empire from Yao. Do you really think that I have gone too far?"

64、孟子访管仲墓

秋高气爽,孟子带着弟子们来到青山环绕的管仲墓前凭吊。孟子想以古人来教导弟子,没想

孟子的故事

到弟子们对老师的行动有所误会。因为齐宣王在雪宫和孟子彻夜长谈，而齐宣王就是希望孟子能像管仲辅佐齐桓公一样辅佐自己登上天下盟主的地位。所以，公孙丑问老师："您如果在齐国当政，能够建立像管仲、晏子一样的功业吗？"孟子说："你真是一个齐国人，只晓得管仲、晏子。"公孙丑说："管仲辅佐齐桓公称霸诸侯，晏子辅佐齐景公名扬天下。难道管仲、晏子不值得学习吗？"孟子说："以当时齐国的实力统一天下，易如反掌。"公孙丑说："照你这样说，我就更不懂了。像周文王那样的德行，而且活了将近一百岁，还没有统一天下，现在您把统一天下说得这样容易，那连周文王也不值得效法了吗？"孟子说："谁能和周文王相比呢？当时的情况不一样，文王时，商朝还很强大，还有不少贤臣辅佐纣王，而当时周国不过是一个百里小国。现在情况不一样了，齐国的强大只须实行仁政就能统一天下。"（《孟子·公孙丑上》）

One clear autumn day, Mencius took his disciples to visit the tomb of Guan Zhong, set in lush green mountains. He wanted to teach them by drawing lessons from the past. But they misunderstood him. They knew that Mencius had had an overnight talk with Duke Xuan at the Snow Palace, and the duke wanted Mencius to help him achieve hegemony.

Gongsun Chou asked his master: "If you served Duke Xuan, could you achieve as much as Guan Zhong and Yan Zi?" Mencius asked, "Do you think I would like to follow in the footsteps of Guan Zhong and Yan Zi?" Gongsun Chou said, "Guan Zhong helped Duke Huan of Qi achieve hegemony, and Yan Zi helped Duke Jing of Qi obtain fame. Is it not worthwhile to learn from them?" Mencius replied, "It was very easy to dominate the world with the strength of Qi at that time." Gongsun Chou was confused. "But Duke Wen of Zhou wasn't able to dominate the world even though he lived to be almost 100 years old. Is he not worth learning from?" Mencius said, "Who can compare himself with Duke Wen? At that time, the Shang Dynasty was still very powerful, while Zhou was a rather small state. Now it is different. The State of Qi is powerful enough to unify the world, so long as it applies a policy of benevolence."

65、孟子谈浩然之气

在孟门弟子中,公孙丑是以武功著称的。有一次孟子和弟子们谈勇气的培养,公孙丑问:"老

师长于哪一方面?"孟子说:"我善于培养我的浩然之气。"公孙丑又问:"什么叫浩然之气呢?"孟子说:"其为气也,至大至刚,用正义去培养它,不能稍有伤害,这种气就会存在于天地之间,无所不在。这种气还必须和义与道相配合,否则就没有什么力量了。"(《孟子·公孙丑上》)

Of all Mencius' disciples, Gongsun Chou excelled in martial arts. Once, when Mencius was discussing courage with his disciples, Gongsun Chou asked him: "What are you good at?" Mencius said, "I'm good at cultivating the great moral force." Gongsun Chou asked again: "What is this great moral force?" Mencius answered, "This force is both wide and strong. If cultivated with justice and not harmed in any way, it will fill the universe. This force exists in harmony with justice and nature. Without them it will lose its power."

66、孟子谈公卿

齐宣王召孟子进宫,问他:"君臣关系如何相处?"孟子说:"君主视臣下如手足,臣下就会视

君主为腹心;君主视臣下如狗马,臣下就会视君主如常人;君主视臣下如泥土草芥,臣下就会视君主如仇敌。"又说:"君主仁,则无人不仁;君主义,则无人不义。"(《孟子·离娄下》)

One day Duke Xuan summoned Mencius to his palace, and asked him about the relationship between a duke and his ministers. Mencius said, "If the duke treats his ministers as his hands and feet, they will take him as their heart and bosom. If the duke treats his ministers as horses and dogs, his ministers will take him as a commoner. If the duke treats his ministers as soil and dirt, his ministers will take him as an enemy...If the duke is benevolent, no one will be unkind. If the duke is just, no one dares to be unjust."

67、孟子谈"三宝"

孟子对齐宣王说:"诸侯有三宝:土地,人民和政治。如果以珍珠美玉为宝,一定会祸及其

身。"(《孟子·尽心上》)

Mencius told Duke Xuan: "For a ruler of a state, there are three treasures: land, people and government. If he takes pearls and jade as the most valuable things, he is inviting disaster."

68、没有规矩不能成方圆

孟子对齐宣王说:"即使有离娄的视力,公输般的技巧,如果不借助于工具,也不能画出标准

的方和圆。"离娄：相传为黄帝时人，目力极强，能于百步之外看清秋毫之末。公输子：名般（一作"班"），鲁国人，又称鲁班。为中国古代著名的能工巧匠。

孟子又说："规矩是方圆的准则，圣人是做人的准则。作为君主，应尽君主之道；作为臣子，应尽臣子之道。二者只要取法尧和舜就行了。不以舜事尧的态度和方法服事君主，便是对君主的不敬；君主不以尧治理百姓的态度和方法治理百姓，便是害民。孔子说过：'治理国家的方法有两种，行仁政和不行仁政罢了。'害民政治，重则身亡国灭；轻则身危国弱。"（《孟子·离娄上》）

"Even if one had eyesight as keen as Li Lou's and the skill of Lu Ban (a famous master carpenter)," Mencius told Duke Xuan, "one could not draw a proper circle and square without the proper tools. The compass and T-square form the criteria of circles and squares. Sages are the criteria of human beings. Both the duke and his subjects should observe their proper ways by following Yao and Shun. Not to serve one's ruler in the way Yao served Shun is to be lacking respect. Not to govern one's state in the way of Yao is to harm the people. Confucius once said, 'There are two ways to govern a state: by being or not being benevolent.' If a ruler treats his people badly, he will ruin his state and meet his doom. Even if he is less harsh, he will still endanger his life and weaken his state."

69、天时不如地利

孟子对齐宣王说:"天时不如地利,地利不如人和。三里之城,七里之郭,环而攻之而不胜。

孟子的故事

夫环而攻之，必有得天时者矣；然而不胜者，是天时不如地利也。城非不高也，池非不深也，兵革非不坚利也，米粟非不多也；委而去之，是地利不如人和也。故曰：域民不以封疆之界，固国不以山豀之险，威天下不以兵革之利。得道者多助，失道者寡助。寡助之至，亲戚畔之；多助之至，天下顺之。以天下之所顺，攻亲戚之所畔；故君子有不战，战必胜矣。"（《孟子·公孙丑下》）

天时、地利、人和：是当时成语，而其内容时有所变。孟子在这里讲的天时是指阴晴寒暑之是否与攻战有利，地利则指高城深池、山川险阻，人和则指人心所向。

Mencius told Duke Xuan: "Favorable weather is less important than advantageous terrain. Advantageous terrain is less important than unity among the people. For instance, a small city besieged for a long time is still not conquered. Even if there is good weather, the enemy can not break into it because favorable weather is not as important as advantageous terrain. Even with high city walls, deep ditches, sturdy weapons and abundant grain, the defenders flee right after the enemy's attack. So, advantageous terrain is not as important as unity among the people. National borders alone cannot bind people to their state, precipitous terrain alone cannot keep the state secure, and military force alone cannot conquer the world. Only a benevolent government can win the support of the people. If one loses the support of the people, even one's relatives will be against him. However, if one wins the support of the people, all the people in the world will come to pay allegiance to him. When a gentleman with the support of the people attacks one deserted by his people, he is sure to win even without fighting."

70、孟子见夷之

墨家信徒夷之通过徐辟求见孟子,孟子则以身体原因推辞不见,对弟子徐辟说:"听说夷子是

墨家信徒，墨家主张薄葬，想以此移风易俗。可是夷子对自己的父母却实行厚葬，这是为什么？"徐辟把老师的话转告夷子，夷子说："我们墨家主张'兼爱'，儒家不是以为古之圣贤爱民如爱其子吗？"孟子听徐辟讲述夷子的观点后说："我们主张'老吾老，以及人之老'这和墨家主张的'爱无差等'是不同的。难道夷子真的认为爱自己的父母和爱别人的父母没有差别吗？"徐辟把孟子的话告诉夷子，夷子怅然良久，喟然叹曰："孟夫子的话使我深明大义。"夷子以后放弃了墨家的观点，改学儒家。（《孟子·滕文公上》）

Yi Zhi, a scholar of the Mohist school, asked Mencius' disciple Xu Pi to secure an interview for him with his master. On the excuse of illness, Mencius declined to meet him, and said to Xu Pi, "I have heard that Yi Zhi believes in Mohism, which advocates frugal burial. But he gave his parents lavish funerals. Why?" When Xu Pi reported these words to Yi Zhi, the latter said, "We believe in love without discrimination. Don't you Confucians think that the ancient sage kings treated people as their own children?" Mencius' comment was "We wish to extend our respect for our parents to others' parents, and that is different from the Mohists' love without discrimination. Does Yi Zhi really think that love for one's own parents and for others' parents is the same?"

When Xu Pi told him what Mencius had said, Yi Zhi sighed, and said, "Mencius has enlightened me." Later, Yi Zhi left the Mohist school and became a Confucian.

71、桃应问执法

弟子桃应问孟子道:"舜做天子,皋陶做法官,假如舜的父亲瞽瞍杀了人,那会怎么办?"孟

子说:"把他逮捕起来就是了。""舜不会阻止吗?""他怎么能阻止呢?皋陶逮捕他父亲是有法可依的。""要是那样,舜又该怎么办呢?"孟子说:"他会像抛弃一只烂鞋一样毫不犹豫地离开天子之位,然后偷偷地背着父亲逃走,在海边住下来,一辈子快快乐乐,把曾做过天子的事忘得一干二净。"(《孟子·尽心上》)

Mencius' disciple Tao Ying consulted Mencius, saying, "Shun was an emperor, and Gaoyao was a judge. Suppose Shun's father killed a man. What should have been done?" Mencius said, "Gaoyao should have arrested him."

"Would Shun have interfered to stop him arresting his father?" asked Tao Ying.

"No. For Gaoyao would have been fully justified."

"Then what should have Shun done?"

Mencius said, "He should have given up his throne like discarding a worn shoe, and secretly carried his father to the seashore. He would have stayed there happily for the rest of his life, completely forgetting that he had once been an emperor."

The Life and Wisdom of Mencius

72、孟子谈孝

桃应对老师所讲舜的孝道有些不能理解,就又问道:"您说舜既然如此大孝,那为什么他不告诉父母就娶尧的两个女儿呢?"孟子说:"你没有

听说过吗?不孝有三,无后为大。舜若先告诉父母,就娶不了妻子,就会断了子嗣,因此君子并不认为舜有什么不对。"(《孟子·离娄上》)

After Mencius talked about filial piety, Tao Ying asked, "If, as you say, Shun was a most filial son, why did he marry the two daughters of Yao without asking his parents' permission?" Mencius said, "Haven't you heard about the three ways of being a bad son? The worst is to have no heir. If Shun's parents had refused their permission, he would not have married his wife and had an heir. So gentlemen did not think he was wrong."

73、孟子讲"四心"

孟子说:"人皆有不忍人之心。先王有不忍人之心斯有不忍人之政矣。以不忍人之心,行不忍

孟子的故事

人之政,治天下可运之掌上。"他又说:"由此看来,一个人如果没有同情心,简直就不是人了。如果没有羞耻之心、谦让之心、是非之心,也就不配为人了。同情心是仁的萌芽,羞耻心是义的萌芽,谦让心是礼的萌芽,是非心是智的萌芽。人有这四种心和有四肢一样是与生俱来的。"(《孟子·公孙丑上》)

Mencius said, "Everyone has a heart of mercy. The ancient sage kings were merciful, and so their governments were merciful. With a heart of mercy and practicing policies of mercy, it will be really easy to run a state. So if one has no sense of sympathy, he is not a human being. Without a sense of shame, modesty and justice, one is not human. Benevolence comes from sympathy; justice comes from a sense of shame; politeness comes from modesty; and wisdom finds its source in righteousness. These four senses come as natural to one as one's four limbs."

74、杯水车薪

孟子对齐宣王说:"仁之胜不仁也,犹水胜火。今之为仁者,犹以一杯水救一车薪之火也;

不熄，则谓之水不胜火，此又与于不仁之甚者也，亦终必亡而已矣。"（《孟子·告子上》）

Mencius said to Duke Xuan: "Just as water can put out fire, so benevolence can overcome cruelty. But it is obviously not enough to try to douse a burning cartload of wood with just one cup of water. Nowadays, people who claim to practice the policy of benevolence are behaving just like that. They claim that water cannot quench fire, and no longer believe in the power of benevolence. So they have joined the ranks of the unrighteous, and what they have achieved in the course of their benevolence has been lost."

75、孟子反对杨、墨学说

有一次公都子对孟子说:"别人都说您好辩,请问这是为什么?"孟子说:"我难道好辩吗? 我

是不得已呀。"孟子从人类社会的发展讲起，一直讲到周文王、周武王灭商纣，使天下太平。他接着又说："后来，太平盛世和王道又逐渐衰落，邪说暴行又沉渣泛起。臣杀君、子杀父，大逆不道的事也时有发生。孔子深为犹虑，于是著《春秋》一书。这本是天子的事，孔子是不得已而为之。所以，孔子说：'了解我的，怕是因为《春秋》这部书；责怪我的，怕也是因为《春秋》这部书。'后来，圣王久不出现，诸侯便肆无忌惮，一般读书人也乱发议论，杨朱、墨翟的学说充斥天下。所有的主张不是属于杨朱派，就是属于墨翟派。杨派主张个人第一，这就否定了应对君上尽忠，就是目无君上。墨家主张天下同仁，不分亲疏，这就否定了对父母尽孝，就是目无父母。目无君上，目无父母，那就成了禽兽了。杨、墨学说不灭亡，孔子学说就无法发扬光大。这就是荒谬的学说欺骗了百姓，从而阻塞了仁义正道。正道被阻，也就等于率领野兽来吃人，人与人之间也将互相残杀。我因此而忧虑，于是便出来捍卫古代圣人的学说，反对杨、墨的学说，驳斥错误的言论，使宣扬荒谬邪说的人不能得势。我也是不得已而为之呀。"（《孟子·滕文公下》）

Once, Gong Duzi asked Mencius: "Why do people say that you are fond of debating?" Mencius replied, "Am I? I can't help it." Then he talked about the history of mankind, about how Duke Wen and Duke Wu overthrew Duke Zhou of Shang and brought peace to the world. He continued, "Later, the peace was broken and the way of good rule waned. All kinds of heresies and cruelty emerged,

with subjects killing their sovereign and sons killing their parents. Confucius was deeply worried about this state of affairs, and wrote the *Spring and Autumn Annals*. It was really the emperor's business to write such a record, but Confucius had to do it. He said, 'Some people will understand me through it, and others will blame me for it.'

"Later, as no more sage rulers appeared, the feudal lords ran wild, and scholars advocated all kinds of nonsensical ideas. The ideologies of Yang Zhu and Mo Zhai were prevalent. Yang Zhu's views were self-centered, negating loyalty to the ruler. Mo Zhai advocated love without discrimination, discarding filial piety. One is no different from the birds and the beasts if one has no sense of loyalty and filial piety. When these absurd ideas fooled people, the road to benevolence and righteousness was blocked, and it was the same as leading animals to devour people or to make people kill each other. If the schools of Yang and Mo are not silenced, Confucius' ideas can not be promoted. I am so worried that I have to speak out to defend the ideas of the ancient sages and refute heresies so that their advocators will not come to power. This is what I have to do."

76、箪食壶浆，以迎王师

公元前 316 年，孟子七十四岁。这一年燕国发生了政变，燕王哙在内外势力的逼迫下，废太子，

把王位禅让给宰相子之。这件事引起了燕国内乱，这时有人劝齐宣王兴兵伐燕，但也有人反对吞并燕国。齐宣王早有霸天下的野心，他认为这是天赐良机，不可错过。他问孟子可不可以出兵？孟子说："取之而燕民悦，则取之。古之人有行之者，武王是也。取之而燕民不悦，则勿取。古之人有行之者，文王是也。以万乘之国伐万乘之国，箪食壶浆，以迎王师，岂有他哉？避水火也。如水益深，如火益热，亦运而已矣。"（《孟子·梁惠王下》）

In 316 BC, when Mencius was 74 years old, Duke Kuai of Yan was forced to hand over the throne to the prime minister, Zi Zhi, instead of to the crown prince, and the State of Yan sank into disorder.

Someone urged Duke Xuan to seize the opportunity to annex Yan. The duke asked Mencius for his advice, and Mencius said, "If the people of Yan would welcome the annexation, you may annex Yan. In fact, in ancient times Duke Wu of Zhou used to do exactly that. But do not annex it if the people would not be happy for you to do so. Duke Wen of Zhou also set such an example. If a dukedom of ten thousand chariots like Qi attacks Yan, a state of the same strength, and the people welcome your army with wine and rice, that means you have liberated them. But if the annexation brings more suffering to the people, it will only be a change of name, not a change in the people's life."

77、齐国灭燕

孟子是赞成齐宣王伐燕的,果然十万齐军所向披靡,只五十日直取燕都,大获全胜。孟子本

来对齐宣王这次军事行动抱有很大的希望，他认为这是齐宣王兴仁义之师称王天下的好时机，希望齐宣王效法周文王、周武王吊民伐罪，救天下百姓于水深火热之中，从而推行仁政于天下。

The powerful Qi army swept forward victoriously, and within 50 days the capital of Yan was captured. Mencius supported this action, and thought that it was a good opportunity for Duke Xuan to lead his army of justice to unify the world. He hoped the duke would follow the examples of Duke Wen and Duke Wu in punishing tyranny and relieve the people of their sufferings, so that benevolence would be practiced the world over.

However, Duke Xuan of Qi was only ambitious to dominate the world. He cared nothing for ruling with benevolence.

78、各诸侯国以救燕的名义讨伐齐国

齐国吞并燕国,引起各诸侯国的强烈不满,商量着联合以救燕的名义讨伐齐国。齐宣王赶紧

The Life and Wisdom of Mencius

向孟子请教。孟子说:"我听说过商汤以七十里小国统一天下,没听说过拥有千里国土的大国而害怕别国的。本来,燕国的君主虐待百姓,你去征伐他,那里的老百姓以为你能把他们从水深火热的苦难中解救出来,所以他们送饭送酒慰劳齐军。而你呢却杀死他们的父兄,掳掠他们的子弟,毁坏他们的宗庙,掠走他们国家的宝器。这怎么能行呢?天下各国本来就害怕齐国强大,现在齐国吞并了燕国,土地扩大了一倍,而且更加暴虐无道,这自然会招致各国要攻伐齐国了。"齐宣王听孟子的话虽不顺耳却很有道理,就赶紧问有什么救急办法。孟子说:"你应该赶快发布命令,遣返燕国俘虏,停止掠夺燕国的宝器,再和燕国有关人士商量,择立新燕王,然后从燕国撤军,这样做好像还来得及使各国停止对齐国兴师问罪。"(《孟子·梁惠王下》)

Qi's annexation of Yan caused resentment among the other states, some of which conspired to form a coalition against Qi. Duke Xuan anxiously consulted Mencius. Mencius said, "I have heard that Duke Tang of Shang, a small state of only 70 li, unified the world, but not that a big state of a thousand li should be afraid of other states. The ruler of Yan was cruel. So when you overthrew him the people there welcomed you warmly in the hope that you would relieve them from their sufferings. But what did you do? You slaughtered people there, destroyed their temples and took their state treasures away! The other states have long feared that Qi might become powerful. Now, with the annexation of Yan, Qi's territory has doubled, and as a consequence it is regarded by the other states as even more threatening. No wonder they have banded together against you!"

Although he was not happy to hear this, Duke Xuan was convinced that Mencius was right, so he hastened to ask if there was any remedy for the situation. Mencius said, "You should send all the captives back home immediately, put a halt to the plundering of treasures from Yan, consult with the people concerned in Yan to select a new ruler for that state, and withdraw your army from Yan. Only by doing so might you stop the other states from ganging up against Qi."

79、齐宣王说：
"我愧对孟子"

齐宣王虽然认为孟子的话不无道理，但吃到嘴里的肥肉再吐出来他也是不情愿的。果然，燕

国人群起反抗齐国,外有各诸侯国讨伐齐国声势压力,内有燕国军民拼死反抗,齐军在燕国难以立足,败回齐国。到这时齐宣王才后悔当初没有听孟子的话。他对大夫陈贾说:"我愧对孟子。"陈贾安慰齐宣王道:"王不要自责。在仁和智方面,您和周公相比如何?"齐宣王这点自知之明还是有的,所以他马上说:"哎!这是什么话!我怎能和周公相比呢。"陈贾说:"当时周公使管叔监督殷国,管叔却率殷民造反。这一结果如果周公已经预见到了,却故意让管叔去监督殷国,那是他不仁。如果事出周公预料之外,那是他不智。周公都不能完全做到仁和智,何况你呢?我愿意去向孟子解释。"于是陈贾来见孟子,并以周公派管叔监督殷国的事和齐宣王伐燕的事比兑一番,来为齐王开脱。孟子已经明了他的来意,就说:"周公的失误是合乎情理的,管叔是兄,周公是弟,弟弟怎能对兄长存有戒心呢?古代有仁德的执政者,有错即改;今天的执政者,有了过错,竟将错就错。古代的执政者,他的过错就像日蚀月蚀一样挂在天上,老百姓都看得见。当他们改正以后,老百姓更加敬仰他们。今天的执政者,不仅将错就错,还一定要编造一番假道理来为其错误辩护。"陈贾听了孟子的话深感羞愧,孟子也对齐宣王失去了信心,萌生了离开齐国的念头。(《孟子·公孙丑下》)

Although Duke Xuan could not deny that Mencius was right, he was reluctant to give up something he had gained after long craving for it. Sure enough, the people of Yan rose against the rule of Qi, and all the other states also condemned Qi's action. The Qi army ended up retreating in disgrace. Duke Xuan told his Prime Minister Chen Jia: "I feel ashamed to face Mencius." Chen Jia said, "Please don't blame yourself so much. Aren't you as benevolent and wise as the Duke of Zhou?"

"How can I be compared with him?" Duke Xuan protested.

Chen Jia continued, "Even the Duke of Zhou could not be both benevolent and wise, because he sent Guan Shu to supervise Yin. But Guan Shu led the people there in rebellion. If he had foreseen this and still sent Guan Shu to do so, he would not have been benevolent. If he was not able to foresee this, he was simply unwise. So you do not have to feel uneasy about the catastrophe at Yan. I will explain this to Mencius."

Chen Jia went to see Mencius and cited the example of the Duke of Zhou, in order to exonerate Duke Xuan from blame. Mencius replied, "It was human for the Duke of Zhou to err, because Guan

Shu was his elder brother. How can one be on guard against one's own brother? In ancient times, the benevolent ruler would correct his mistakes because they were seen by all the people——just like solar and lunar eclipses. After he corrected his mistakes, his people admired him all the more. But rulers nowadays leave their mistakes uncorrected. And to make things worse, they even make excuses for them." Chen Jia was deeply ashamed. Mencius was also disillusioned with Duke Xuan and began to feel that he should leave Qi.

The Life and Wisdom of Mencius

80、夫子之道

孟子有了离开齐国的念头后,经常带领弟子出游,有一次他们游历过海滨之后,在乘车回临

淄的路上公孙丑、万章和老师同车。公孙丑说："夫子之道虽然很好,但却像登天一样高不可攀,您为什么不使它容易攀登好让人每天去努力呢?"孟子说:"高明的工匠不会因工人笨拙而改变或废弃规矩,羿也不会因射手拙劣而改变张弓的标准。君子育人就像教人射箭一样,拉满了弓,却不发箭,作出跃跃欲试的样子,自己站在正确的道路上,有能力的人便会跟上来。"(《孟子·尽心上》)

Once, on their way back from a trip to the seashore, Mencius' disciple Gongsun Chou said to him: "Your principles are excellent, but they are as hard to practice as the sky is to reach. Why don't you make them easier, so that more people can try to practice them every day?" Mencius said, "A good craftsman will not change or give up his rules to make things easier for clumsy workers. Nor would Yi lower his standards for archery for the sake of poor marksmen. Just like Yi taught archery, a gentleman teaches people by drawing the bow to the full. Yet he doesn't discharge the arrow just to show his eagerness to shoot. When he stands in the right road, others capable enough will follow him."

81、孟子准备离开齐国

孟子七十八岁这一年,齐国伐燕失败后,齐国朝廷矛盾激化。齐国内乱大有一触即发之势,孟子决心不再过问齐国的政治,也不再向齐宣王

提及实行仁政的话。一心研究学问，教诲弟子并着手和弟子们整理资料，闲下来就去拜访朋友，作离开齐国的准备。

In Mencius' 78th year, the strife in the court of Qi intensified after Qi's failure to annex Yan. Mencius decided to distance himself from the politics of Qi, and stop trying to convert Duke Xuan to the rule of benevolence. He busied himself with his research, teaching and sorting out records with his disciples. He was already making preparations to leave Qi.

82、孟子称病不朝

孟子写好辞职奏章正想送进宫去,正巧齐宣王派人来访,对孟子说:"大王本欲亲来看望夫

子,但不巧病了,怕受风,所以不能来了。如果夫子肯去朝拜,大王将很高兴接见您。"孟子说:"不巧的很,我也病了,不能到朝廷中来。"其实,孟子并没有病,只是他已经不想再见齐宣王。景丑不明白孟子的心意,就问他说:"在家有父子,在朝有君臣,这是人与人之间最重要的关系。父子间讲慈爱,君臣间讲恭敬,齐王听说你病了,就立即派人来看你,而你本来也想去看齐王,可是一听说齐王召见,你反而不去了,这是为什么?"孟子说:"大家公认尊贵者有三:爵位,年龄,道德。在朝廷论爵位高低;在乡里论年龄大小;至于辅助君主治理国家自然以道德为上。他怎么能以爵位来轻视我的年龄和道德呢?所以,对有些臣子君主是不可以随便召唤的。君主有事应该亲自到臣子那里去请教。如果君主不能崇尚道德和乐行仁政,便不足与他共事。商汤对于伊尹,齐桓公对于管仲,都是先以师事之,然后才以他们为臣。虽然如此,商汤和齐桓公都不敢随便召唤他们。连管仲都不能随便召唤,何况连管仲也看不起的人呢?"(《孟子·公孙丑下》)

Just as Mencius was about to announce his resignation from the court, a messenger from Duke Xuan came and said to him: "The Duke meant to visit you personally, but was unfortunately sick, and couldn't come. If you could go to court, he would be happy to give you an audience." Mencius replied, "Unfortunately I'm sick too, and can't go to court." Actually this was just an excuse, because he did not want to see the duke any more.

Jing Chou asked him why he had refused to see the duke. Mencius said, "There are three things that are generally accepted as valuable: a noble title, age and morality. At court, a noble title is most valuable; in one's neighborhood, age is most respected; but in helping the duke to rule the state, it is morality that is most important. How could he look down on my age and morality just because he is the ruler? Some officials should not be summoned casually. The duke should go to seek their advice in person about important matters. If the duke does not value morality and refuses to practice a policy of benevolence, he is not worthy of service. Tang, the ruler of Shang, took Yi Yin as his tutor first before using him as his official, as did Duke Huan of Qi with Guan Zhong. Even so, Tang and Duke Huan dared not summon Yi Yin and Guan Zhong casually."

83、君子不见诸侯

孟子避齐宣王召而不见,不仅景丑弄不明白,连弟子们也弄不明白。公孙丑问孟子:"君子不谒

见诸侯,有什么道理?"孟子说:"君子不是不可以谒见诸侯,如果诸侯一定要见你,也是可以见的。但诸侯必须是诚心诚意依礼相见。不能像阳货欲见孔子那样采用欺诈的手腕。我最不赞成勉强自己陪着笑脸去见自己讨厌的人。"(《孟子·滕文公下》)

Not only Jing Chou, but none of Mencius' disciples understood why he had avoided seeing Duke Xuan of Qi, so Gongsun Chou asked him the reason. Mencius said, "It is not that a gentleman should keep a ruler at a distance absolutely. If the ruler insists on summoning you, you may go and see him. But the audience should be held sincerely and appropriately, not out of trickery, as Yang Huo tricked Confucius. The one thing I hate most is to force a smile when I see someone I dislike."

84、志士不忘在沟壑，勇士不忘丧其元

弟子陈代也对孟子说："您不去谒见诸侯，似乎只是拘泥于小节。现在齐宣王这样看重您，您

如果去见他，大可以帮助齐国实行仁政，统一天下；小可以革新政治，称霸中国。大丈夫能伸能缩，正应该大干一场。"孟子说："从前齐景公田猎，用不合礼法的方法召唤猎场管理官员，该官员竟不予理会，齐景公准备将他治罪，可是他并不畏惧。孔子曾称赞过他'志士不忘在沟壑，勇士不忘丧其元。'孔子称赞他什么呢？就称赞他敢于依礼办事的精神。假如我抛开自己的政治主张和志向而主动去追随诸侯那又算什么呢？你错了，己不正焉能正人。"（《孟子·滕文公下》）

Another disciple, Chen Dai, said, "It seems that you are being too stubborn not to call on the duke, who holds you in high esteem. If you go to see him, you can help Qi unify the empire with your policy of benevolence, or at least you can help him to reform his government and achieve hegemony. You should be more flexible, and help him out." Mencius said, "Once, Duke Jing of Qi went hunting. He sent an improper summons to the gamekeeper, who refused to respond. Duke Jing wanted to execute him for insubordination, but the fearless gamekeeper pointed out the duke's lack of propriety, and was spared. Confucius highly praised him as 'a hero who would not hesitate to leave his corpse in the wilderness in defense of his lofty ideals, and a warrior who would do what was right even at the risk of his life.' So why should I lay aside my political ideals to cringe before the duke? No one in the wrong can correct others who are adamant in their errors."

85、齐宣王挽留孟子

齐宣王得知孟子执意离去,又不肯入朝见驾,就亲自到稷下看望孟子,说:"昔者愿见夫子而不

可得，后得为君臣而同朝，今夫子又弃寡人而归，不知日后何时才得相见。"齐宣王不愿接受孟子的仁政主张，但对孟子还是很尊重的。孟子也客气地说："实不敢当，我想还是有机会的吧。"

齐宣王为了挽留孟子对时子说："寡人欲在临淄为孟子造一处府邸，以万钟之粟养其弟子，使齐之诸大夫及国人均有所效法。子何不为寡人言之！"（《孟子·公孙丑下》）

When Duke Xuan learned that Mencius was determined to leave the State of Qi, and would not come to court to see him, he personally went to the Jixia School to see Mencius. "I used to long to see you but couldn't. I was happy that we could work together in the court for some time. Now you are forsaking me. Will we have the chance to meet again?" Although Duke Xuan would not adopt Mencius' ideas of benevolence, he was very respectful to him. Mencius said, "I dare not ask for such a favor, but I wish we could."

After the visit, Duke Xuan said to Shi Zi: "I want to build a mansion for Mencius here in the capital, Linzi, provide ten thousand *zhong* of grain for his disciples and make him an example for my officials and people to follow. Will you tell this to Mencius for me?" We can see from this that the duke was really sincere about keeping Mencius in his state.

86、淳于髡挽留孟子

齐宣王为了挽留孟子,又让淳于髡去作说服工作。淳于髡在齐国以能言善辩有名,并且曾和孟子多次辩论。虽然齐王的本意是让他设法挽留

孟子,而他却并不想孟子常留在齐国。所以,他一见孟子就说:"重视名誉功业,是为了济世救民;轻视名誉功业,是为了独善其身。您身为齐国三卿之一,上辅君王,下济臣民,名誉功业还未能建立就急于离开齐国,仁人难道应该这样吗?"孟子说:"仁人辅佐君王目的只有一个,就是实行仁政。如果君主不能实行仁政,就应该离开朝廷。"孟子对他讲了伊尹、伯夷、柳下惠和孔子的故事。(《孟子·告子下》)

Duke Xuan of Qi also asked Chuyu Kun, an eloquent speaker who had had several debates with Mencius, to try to persuade Mencius to stay in Qi. Chunyu Kun, however, was not keen for Mencius to stay for long in Qi. He said to Mencius: "People who deem achievement as important aim at benefiting the people and the state. People who take achievement lightly pay more attention to their own moral uplifting. As one of the three most important ministers of the state, you want to leave without either helping the duke or benefiting the people. Is that the right course for a benevolent person?"

Mencius replied, "The aim of a benevolent person in assisting a ruler is to guide him toward a policy of benevolence. If the ruler is unwilling to adopt such a policy, the advisor should leave the court." Then Mencius cited the examples of Yiyin, Boyi, Liuxia Hui and Confucius in support of his argument.

87、要用"道"去援救天下

淳于髡问："男女授受不亲,这是礼制吗?"孟子说："是礼制。""那么,如果眼看着嫂嫂掉到水里,可以用手去拉她吗?""看见嫂嫂掉到水里而

不去拉她，这简直是豺狼。男女之间授受不亲，这是常礼。看到嫂嫂掉到水里用手去拉她，这是变通的办法。"淳于髡马上反问道："现在天下人都掉到了水里，您不去援救，又是为什么呢？"孟子说："天下人都掉到水里了，要用'道'去援救；嫂嫂掉到水里，用手去援救。你难道要我用一双手去援救天下人吗？"（《孟子·离娄上》）

Chanyu Kun asked Mencius: "Do the rites forbid men and women to have physical contact with each other?" Mencius said, "Yes." The other then said, "In that case, if your sister-in-law were drowning, would it be permissible for you to stretch out your hand to save her?" Mencius answered, "It would be inhuman if one did not. Though the rites forbid physical contact between men and women, in the case of a drowning sister-in-law, reaching out a hand to save her is allowed."

"But now, all the people in the world are drowning. Why don't you rush to save them?" Chanyu Kun lost no time asking again. Mencius said, "If all the people in the world are drowning, they should be saved with the Dao. A drowning sister-in-law should be saved with the hand. Could you expect me to save the whole world with my hand?"

88、孟子离开齐国

深秋一日,秋雨中孟子师徒的车马离开稷下学宫,大街之上,送行的人群站满两厢,其中有

各级官吏，也有布衣百姓。

One rainy day in late autumn, Mencius and his disciples left the Jixia School in a long line of carriages. People crowded both sides of the road to see them off. Among the bystanders were officials of all levels, as well as common people....

89、如欲平治天下,当今之世,舍我其谁也?

孟子一行离开齐国,在路上弟子充虞问:"您的样子好像很不高兴,您从前说过'君子不怨天

尤人'现在为什么这样呢?"孟子说:"彼一时,此一时也。时势不同,情况也随之变化。从历史来看,每过五百年就一定会有圣君兴起,也一定会有仁人出来辅佐圣君。从周武王以来已经七百多年了,无论从年数还是从时势上讲,都应该有圣君贤臣出世平定天下的时候。这是上天不愿使天下平定吧;如欲平治天下,当今之世,舍我其谁也?"(《孟子·公孙丑下》)

On their way from the State of Qi, Mencius' disciple Ziyu asked him: "You once told us that a gentleman should blame neither Heaven nor Earth. So, why do you look unhappy?"

Mencius said, "Things change with time. History shows that a sage ruler emerges every 500 years, who will be assisted by wise men. It has been 700 years since the age of Duke Wu of Zhou, and so it is high time for another sage ruler to arise. Maybe it is not God's will to keep the world at peace now. But if it is, who else but I can do it?"

The Life and Wisdom of Mencius

90、孟子在昼地

孟子师徒离开齐国,在昼地过夜。有一个想为齐宣王挽留孟子的人很恭敬地和孟子说话,孟

子却靠几假睡,那人很不高兴,孟子对他说:"齐宣王根本没有实行仁政的思想,所以他连一般君主对待贤人的礼节都作不到,而你却以几句空话挽留我有什么意思呢?"(《孟子·公孙丑下》)

Mencius and his disciples stayed in Zhou on their way out of the State of Qi. A messenger came from Duke Xuan of Qi to plead with him to return. But Mencius showed no interest, and dozed off against a table. The envoy was much offended. Mencius explained, "Duke Xuan does not want to practice a policy of benevolence at all, so he can not treat virtuous men in the way that a sovereign should. So what is the point of all your pleas for me to stay?"

91、孟子答尹士

孟子离开齐国这件事,在齐国朝野引起很大的反响。有一个叫尹士的齐国人对孟子的弟子高子说:"如果当初看不透齐王做不了商汤、周武王

那样的圣君,是孟子无识人之明;如果已经看透了齐王不行,自己还来齐国做官,那便是贪图富贵。现在看出齐王不行就离开齐国,可是却在昼地住了三天才动身,为什么还这样恋恋不舍呢?"高子把这话告诉孟子。孟子说:"我老远的来见齐王,是抱着很大希望的。现在离开实在是不得已呀!我在昼地住了三天才离开,正是我还对齐王抱有幻想,总希望齐王能改变态度,派人追我回去。齐王虽然不能成为商汤、周武王那样的圣君,也是可以成就一番事业的。一直到现在我仍然盼望着齐王能改变态度。"尹士听了这番话,感叹道:"我这是以小人之心度君子之腹呀!"(《孟子·公孙丑下》)

Yin Shi said to Mencius' disciple Gao Zi: "Mencius is not wise if he can not see that the ruler of Qi can never be like Shang Tang or Zhou Wu. If he knew that, then he came to Qi simply to seek rank and wealth. Now he has left Qi because he is disappointed with Duke Xuan. But why has he been lingering in Zhou for three days? Is it that he is still reluctant to leave?" When Mencius heard this, he said, "I came to Duke Xuan full of great expectations. But now I have no choice but to leave. I have remained in Zhou for three days because I was hoping that the duke would change his mind. He could achieve something, though he could never be another Shang Tang or Zhou Wu. Even now, I wish that the duke would change his mind." Hearing this, Yin Shi sighed, and said, "Then I have been measuring the stature of a great man with the yardstick of a small man."

92、孟子石丘遇宋牼

孟子师徒离开齐国回邹国去，路过宋国石丘正好碰见宋牼要到楚国去。当时秦楚两国正在打

仗，他告诉孟子他要以战争对两国都不利去劝说两国君主休兵罢战。孟子对他说："先生的志向是不错的，可先生的提法却不行。不能以利害去游说两国君主，只能以仁义去劝说两国君主罢战。"（《孟子·告子下》）

On their way from the State of Qi to the State of Zou, Mencius and his disciples met Song Geng in the State of Song. Song Geng was heading for the State of Chu. At that time, Qin and Chu were at war. Song Geng told Mencius that he would try to explain to the sovereigns of Qin and Chu that the war could bring benefit to neither of them, and thus persuade them to cease hostilities. Mencius said, "You have good intentions, but your argument won't work. You shouldn't talk about benefit. You can only persuade them by using the concepts of benevolence and righteousness."

93、孟子在休地

孟子离开齐国后,一天住在休地。公孙丑问:"做官而不受禄,合乎古道吗?"孟子说:"不是这

样的。我们上次回到齐国在崇地我第一次看见齐宣王时就已经知道他不能实行仁道,我就决计离开齐国,所以我不愿接受齐王的俸禄。后来不久,齐国发生了战事,不能马上离开。留在齐国这么久,不是我的本意。"(《孟子·公孙丑下》)

After leaving the State of Qi, one day Mencius stayed at Xiu. Gongsun Chou asked him: "Is it in accord to the ancient way to be an official without accepting the salary?" Mencius said, "No. Actually the first time I saw Duke Xuan of Qi I knew that he was not a person who could practice a policy of benevolence. I didn't want to take the salary, because I had already decided to leave Qi. Yet I couldn't leave when I wanted to, because of the war. It was not my intention to stay there as long as I did."

◇◇◇◇◇◇ 孟子的故事 ◇◇◇◇◇◇

94、孟子回到邹国

公元前312年的九月九日,孟子一行回到邹国,孟子四十三岁离家,七十八岁还乡,在异国

他乡流浪飘泊了三十五年。归国后，孟子先去拜谒父母的坟墓……

On September 9, 312 BC, Mencius and his disciples arrived back in the State of Zou. At that time, Mencius was 78 years old. After wandering in other states for 35 years, the first thing Mencius did upon his return was to visit his parents' tombs...

孟子的故事

95、重整子思书院

子思书院是孟子思想的发祥地,也是他信仰的基础。孟子和当年孔子一样带着一部分弟子周

The Life and Wisdom of Mencius

游列国，而仍有相当的弟子留在家里由掌门弟子或大弟子辅导。孟子这次回来弟子们都非常高兴。从此，孟子再也没有离开过子思书院。

The Zisi School was the birthplace of Mencius' ideas and beliefs. Mencius traveled around the empire with some of his disciples just as Confucius did, but still quite a few of his disciples stayed in the State of Zou, instructed by his senior disciples. They were all delighted to see their master back, and Mencius never left the Zisi School again.

96、和弟子们研究学问

万章问孟子："据说舜娶了尧的两个女儿为妻,却不告诉父母,这是为什么?"孟子说:"男女结合,是人与人关系的根本准则。舜如果事先禀告父母,父母是不会同意的,他们便不能结合,这伦常大道便会在舜身上废弃,所以他没有事先禀告父母。"万章说:"尧把自己的两个女儿给舜

为妻,为什么也不告诉舜的父母呢?"孟子说:"尧也知道如果告诉舜的父母,他们也不会同意的。"万章说:"舜的父母和弟弟象三番五次想害死舜,难道舜一点也不知道吗?他为什么还那样孝顺父母,友爱弟弟呢?难道他脸上的笑容是假装的吗?"孟子就以舜以孝为先的精神教导弟子。

Wan Zhang asked Mencius: "Why is it that Shun married the two daughters of Yao without asking permission from his parents?" Mencius said, "The union of men and women concerns the basic normal human relationships. If he had asked for his parents' permission, and met their objections, he wouldn't have been able to get married and enjoy this normal human relationship." Wan Zhang asked again: "Why didn't Yao inform Shun's parents about Shun's marriage?" Mencius said, "For the same reason. Yao was sure that if Shun's parents had known about it, they would have objected to it."

Wan Zhang was puzzled, "Didn't Shun know that his parents and brother wanted to kill him several times? Why was he so filial to his parents and kind to his brother all the same? Were all his smiles feigned?" Mencius explained that Shun considered filial piety the most important thing.

97、著书立说

万章问:"据传说舜曾在野外向天哭诉,他为什么要这样呢?"孟子说:"由于他对父母既怨恨又怀恋的缘故。"万章说:"曾子说过,无论什么时候都不能对父母怨恨,难道舜怨恨父母吗?"孟

子说:"帝尧让自己的九个儿子和两个女儿都去服事舜,后来又把帝位禅让给他。可是他却始终得不到父母的欢心,因此他一直很忧郁。有的人娶了妻子,便迷恋妻室;做了官,便想方设法讨好君主,得不到君主的欢心,便急得抓耳挠腮。只有最孝顺的人才会终身怀恋父母。帝位和美色都不能消除舜心中的忧愁。"(《孟子·万章上》)

Mencius and his disciples were busy sorting out teaching materials night and day. While they were working on the *Book of Songs* and *Book of Historical Documents*, Wan Zhang said, "I heard that once Shun wept out his grief to Heaven in the field. Why?" Mencius said, "That was because, as a filial son, he still loved his parents." Wan Zhang asked again: "Zeng Zi said, 'One should never bear a grudge against one's parents.' Did Shun do so?" Mencius said, "Emperor Yao let his nine sons and two daughters serve Shun, and passed his crown on to Shun. But Shun was still sad, because he couldn't win his parents' favor. Men love their wives after they get married. They eagerly try every means to win the sovereign's favor once they are officials. But only the most filial son loves his parents all his life. Neither the crown nor beauties can heal his heart."

◇ ◇ ◇ ◇ ◇ ◇ 孟子的故事 ◇ ◇ ◇ ◇ ◇ ◇

98、子产的故事

孟子给弟子们讲了一个子产的故事：从前有一个人给郑国的子产送条活鱼，子产让管理池塘

的人把鱼放进池塘养起来。那人却把鱼煮吃了，还欺骗子产说已经把鱼放回了池塘，子产相信了他，很高兴的样子。那人欺骗了子产，很得意地对人说："谁说子产聪明，我已经把鱼吃了，他还高兴地说'鱼到了个好地方！'"孟子讲完故事又对弟子们说："所以对君子，可以用合乎情理的方法欺骗他，却不能用违反道德的诡诈来迷惘他。"（《孟子·万章上》）

Mencius told his disciples a story: Once a man sent Zi Chan of Zheng a live fish. Zi Chan asked a pond manager to raise it in his pond. But the manager ate it, and lied to Zi Chan that he had put it in the pond. Zi Chan was happy to hear it. The manager was pleased with his trick, and said to people, "Who said that Zi Chan was clever? I ate his fish, but he said happily that the fish had found its place!" Mencius then said to his disciples: "A gentleman can be cheated in reasonable ways, but he cannot be fooled by wicked tricks."

99、孟子溘然长逝

公元前305年十一月十五日早晨,孟子在弟子们扶持下,梳洗穿戴毕,一边对弟子们谆谆叮

嘱,一边调理琴弦,心有所思地抚琴……突然,琴弦"嘣"的一声断了,歌声、琴声戛然而止,孟子泰然自若地溘然长逝。

孔子之后又一位伟大的思想家、政治家、教育家孟子与世长辞,享年八十五岁。

On the morning of November 15, 305 BC, after getting washed and dressed with the help of his disciples, Mencius adjusted the strings of his zither while earnestly advising the disciples on their studies. Then he played the zither as if lost in thought. Suddenly, the string broke, and the music and song stopped all at once. Mencius passed away calmly and painlessly at the age of 85.

Mencius, the greatest thinker and educationist to follow Confucius, departed from the world forever.

100、"亚圣"孟子

孟子善辩，连他的弟子也说他"好辩"，虽然他自己说是"不得已而为之"。毫无疑问，在反对

杨墨诸家之说、弘扬孔子之道方面,孟子的功劳是最大的。也可能正因此,孟子死前身后受到攻伐也最厉害,甚至受到儒家各派的不容。所以,汉以前孟子学派是非常寥落的。唐代以后,由于大文学家、政治家韩愈的推崇,孟子在儒家的地位日隆,上升到几乎和孔子差不多齐名的地位,被称为"亚圣"。

Mencius was a very skillful speaker. His disciples said that he was "fond of debating," though he himself said that he only debated when compelled to do so. Mencius was doubtlessly the greatest defender and promoter of the ideas of Confucius against the schools of Yang Zhu and Mo Zhai. Because of this, he was severely criticized before and after his death, and outside and even within the Confucian school. So before the Han Dynasty his school of thought had a very limited number of followers.

Promoted by the great Tang Dynasty man of letters and politician Han Yu, Mencius' position in the Confucian school rose continuously thereafter, and he was eventually acclaimed as the "Lesser Sage" with a reputation almost as resounding as that of Confucius.

图书在版编目（CIP）数据

孟子的故事/蔡希勤编著；郁苓译.北京:华语教学出版社，2002.6 （中国圣人文化丛书）
ISBN 7－80052－833－2

I.孟… II.①蔡… ②郁… III.英语－对照读物，传记－英、汉 IV.H319.4：K

中国版本图书馆 CIP 数据核字（2002）第 028688 号

孟子的故事

编注 蔡希勤
英译 郁 苓
绘图 李士伋

*

©华语教学出版社
华语教学出版社出版
（中国北京百万庄路24号）
邮政编码 100037
电话:（86）10-68995871
传真:（86）10-68326333
网址:www.sinolingua.com.cn
电子信箱:hyjx@sinolingua.com.cn
北京外文印刷厂印刷
中国国际图书贸易总公司海外发行
（中国北京车公庄西路35号）
北京邮政信箱第399号 邮政编码100044
新华书店国内发行
2002年（34开）第一版
2005年第二次印刷
（汉英）
ISBN 7-80052-833-2 / H.1339（外）
9－CE－3498P
定价：18.00元